the
age of
customer
equity

the
age of
customer
equity

data-driven strategies to build a sustainable company

ALLISON HARTSOE

DATAFORGE  PRESS

PRAISE FOR
THE AGE OF CUSTOMER EQUITY

Put The Age of Customer Equity *on top of your required reading list! Allison Hartsoe has delivered the 'go-to' book on customer-centric marketing and company leadership, showing C-Suite leaders how to use data correctly, and how to listen and learn from customers.*

DAVID MATHISON • CEO at CDO Club/CDO Summit

Allison Hartsoe delivers a fresh perspective on ways that corporate leaders can listen to and learn from customers.

JUNE DERSHEWITZ • Data Strategy at Amazon Music and
Board Chair at Digital Analytics Association

Allison Hartsoe is the industry insider you need in your corner. Her first-hand experience working with dozens of Fortune 500 brands and start-ups is distilled in The Age of Customer Equity.

JOSE A. MURILLO • Chief Analytics Officer at Grupo Financiero Banorte

I've followed Allison's career for more than a decade, and her relentless focus on helping companies discover the value of their customers has been remarkable. This book captures much of what she has observed and learned and presents it in a compelling and actionable form. Even as a student of customer equity myself, I was quickly reminded of how much untapped opportunity remains.

JOE MEGIBOW • CEO at Purple Innovation

Allison Hartsoe understands what it takes to move through each stage of your brand's customer-centric transformation and the ultimate rewards. In The Age of Customer Equity, she provides in-depth insights into the stages of listening, learning, and growing with your customers.

NEIL HOYNE • Chief Measurement Strategist at Google, Senior Fellow at Wharton, Author at Penguin Random House

If you're interested in developing a more customer-centric business, start with this book. Allison Hartsoe's experience and expertise shine through in her case studies, interviews, and concepts.

JAIME COLMENARES • currently Head of Analytics / Marketing Intelligence at Uber, formerly at Airbnb, eBay, and Bain & Company

The Age of Customer Equity is a roadmap to getting to aligning your teams, rethinking your customer acquisitions, and leading your company toward a customer-centric one. In an age where everyone needs to "Be Like Amazon," Allison shows the way.

BRYAN EISENBERG • *New York Times* bestselling author of *Waiting for Your Cat to Bark* and *Be Like Amazon: Even a Lemonade Stand Can Do It*

Don't you think of launching your next product or service before reading The Age of Customer Equity. Without knowing who your customers are, what they need, and what they really want, it's not worth the exercise or the money. Let Allison show you the customer-centric way.

ZACHERY ANDERSON • Chief Data and Analytics Officer at NatWest

Allison Hartsoe knows how companies move through a customer-centric transformation and the massive payoffs they see. In The Age of Customer Equity, she shares the tools you need to listen to, learn from, and grow with your customers.

JEFF NEMETH • Executive Director of Global Ownership Lifecycle at Ford Motor Company

If you want to "walk the walk" and not just "talk the talk" of customer-centricity, Allison Hartsoe's The Age of Customer Equity *delivers clear, concise, practical advice on every aspect of customer-centric marketing and leadership. It's the best guide there is for transforming your enterprise from the way you work now to real customer-centricity.*

GARY ANGEL • CEO at Digital Mortar

Allison Hartsoe, an industry insider who has worked with dozens of Fortune 500 brands, shows exactly how companies attain the maximum possible return on their investment during a customer-centric transformation. In The Age of Customer Equity, *she shares the tools you need to listen to and learn from your customers so that everyone thrives.*

DENISE BROSSEAU • CEO at Thought Leadership Lab

We've always known data was a treasure trove of information, but we never stopped to analyze the depths of its value to businesses everywhere. The game has changed—from eyeballs and ears to hearts and minds, and data is what allows you to make that customer connection even more valuable. As an expert in the field, Allison's book explores how integral customer-centricity has become to increase value and the connection between brands and customers. Data is your conduit; customer satisfaction is your end goal.

JEFFREY HAYZLETT • Primetime TV & Podcast Host, Speaker, Author, and Part-Time Cowboy

Few people have the industry experience and data knowledge that Allison Hartsoe has. In your hands, you're holding a master class on how to take your business from product-centric to customer-centric to become (and stay) a successful and sustainable company.

BROOKS BELL • Founder at Brooks Bell, Board Member, and Serial Entrepreneur

Allison Hartsoe provides an MBA in customer-centric marketing and company leadership.

ANTHONY CHOE • Founder at Provenance

As a true industry insider, Allison Hartsoe has been at the frontlines of the dawning of the Customer Era. In her new book, The Age of Customer Equity, *Allison shows every current and prospective business leader how a customer-centric transformation provides companies with big-time payoffs. Read her book, and acquire the tools you will need to listen to, learn from, and grow with your customers.*

RICHARD WHITT • Founder at Deeper Edge LLC, President at GLIA Foundation, Mozilla Foundation Fellow, and Strategic Advisor to Tech Startups

There's no lack of information or data coming from customers in today's hyperconnected world. And it's in your customer data where you will find the right answers to those hard business decisions. Allison has a unique gift for looking at and reading data in a way that brings it to life. In The Age of Customer Equity, *she lays out the roadmap for you and your teams to learn from, delight, and keep customers coming back.*

PEGGY WINTON • President/CEO at Association for Intelligent Information Management

Moving your company through a customer-centric transformation is no easy feat. It requires listening to your customers, learning from them, and leading with the right data. As leaders, we have to confront the resistance to change, avoid the pits of reporting despairs, and there's no better way of accomplishing that than to do the work. Allison has decades of experience in data analysis and has delivered a master class on going from a product-centric company to a customer-centric one.

RICHARD FOX • Analytics, Business and Data Strategy, Data Science, CAO, CFO, Adjunct Professor

Allison is the first expert I think of when it comes to measuring and maximizing customer lifetime value. She perfectly distills her expertise into a book that is the MBA in customer-centricity every executive sorely needs.

LEA PICA • Data Storytelling and Presentation Advocate, Speaker, Trainer at Story-Driven Data by Lea Pica

For my husband, Hunt, whose unshakable belief
allowed me to reach for the stars.

Dataforge Press, Publisher

Cover and interior design by
Andrew Welyczko • AbandonedWest Creative, Inc.

Book production by Broad Book Group, LLC

ISBN-13: 978-1-7375181-0-5
eISBN: 978-1-7375181-1-2
Library of Congress Control Number: 2021917654

Printed in the United States of America

21 22 23 24 25   10 9 8 7 6 5 4 3 2 1

CONTENTS

CHAPTER 6

What We Could Ultimately Gain

FOREWORD
BY SARAH E. TOMS

WE ARE data obsessed. Which we should be, because data has the potential to reveal so many answers—as long as we are asking the right questions. The good news is that it's never been easier or cheaper to collect vast amounts of information about our customers. But while businesses are more data wealthy than ever before, there's still a disconnect between the products and services they offer and what their customers *actually* want. That's why it's now up to you to go deeper to discover what truly connects you with your ideal customer.

As coauthor of *The Customer Centricity Playbook*, and the serious games expert who architected Wharton Interactive's Customer Centricity Simulation, I spend a lot of time with business leaders from a wide array of industries figuring out how to do just this. And after an intense day immersed in this simulation, I hear the same takeaway from participants over and over again. It goes something like this: "We spend so much time analyzing customer data, but we've been doing this all wrong. We're not producing what our customers want, or driving increased value for our business. But I can now see why pivoting our focus to customer lifetime value (CLV) will be a game changer for our business."

I cofounded Wharton Interactive to build the next generation of business simulations to deliver experiences where learners can be in the driver's seat of the thought leadership we teach at The Wharton School. Delivering aha moments like this one, in game after game. My team is also a lean edtech startup within the larger University of Pennsylvania ecosystem, which means I am challenged daily to practice what I preach. I am invested in making sure every functional area of my team remains keenly focused on the connection to our customers (or learners and educators around the globe, in our case). From product development through testing and support, tracking data that honors the heterogeneous landscape about our customer base is key.

Making the customer the North Star of all we do from product or service ideation to marketing strategy and fulfillment is a concept that a lot of companies pay lip service to, but rarely deliver on. When you don't focus on customer centricity, your company eventually experiences customer churn, high return rates, and you can lose the connection that brought people to you in the first place.

Allison has spent a career developing ways to bridge the gap between the product/service and customers who are loyal to a company's brand. She, along with her team at Ambition Data, dig deeply to help their clients view data not just as numbers and statistics but start seeing it for what it is—customer insight.

Helping your team humanize customer data can allow you to connect with the right customers at the right time. You can go from having a customer base to having a real relationship with your customers. By centering on your customers, information about them will lead the way as you develop products, change how you market to them, and deliver an experience that will connect them not only to your business, but to your brand for the long term. When your customers feel valued, they become part of your brand team.

In your hands you hold the tools and insight you need to understand your customers, build quality relationships with them, and ensure they become lifetime customers. Allison's insight into the ecosystem of customer data and application of customer centricity provide the road map you need to reach a new level of customer engagement.

* * *

Sarah E. Toms *is executive director and cofounder of Wharton Interactive. She is a serious games expert and demonstrated thought leader in the educational technology field, fueled by a passion to find and develop innovative ways to make every learning environment active, engaging, more meaningful, and* *learner-centered. In addition, Sarah is coauthor of* The Customer Centricity Playbook, *the Digital Book Awards 2019 Best Business Book.*

Her drive to modernize, transform, and democratize education led Sarah and her team to co-invent Simpl.cloud, an open-source simulation framework. She has spent more than twenty years as a leader in the technology sphere, and was an entrepreneur for over a decade, founding companies that built global CRM, product development, productivity management, and financial systems. She is dedicated to supporting women and girls in the technology field, cofounding WIT@Penn, and through her work with the Women in Tech Summit and techgirlz.org. Follow her on twitter at @SarahEToms.

INTRODUCTION

A Cautionary Tale: They Saw It Coming

AMONG DATA analysts, there is a well-known story about how Caesars Entertainment casinos got really good at sensing when the customer experience was about to go south. The casino systems watch for a customer who loses too much money too fast. Then, rather than have the customer leave in frustration and risk all the future dollars the customer could have spent at the casino, they send in the "Luck Fairy." The Luck Fairy could be a customer service rep or a text message that sends a little bit of good fortune in the form of $20 dollars off for the buffet, or even concert tickets, thereby turning frustration into fancy.

Caesars analytics leadership clearly understood the value of each customer and how to keep them engaged. They were well ahead of their time in customer analytics, but it was not enough. They could not pivot fast enough to outrun a massive private equity investment that ultimately crippled the company. Caesars filed for bankruptcy in 2015. What is not commonly known, however, is in the midst of bankruptcy proceedings, creditors filed a countersuit. In it, they alleged that Caesars Total Rewards customer data base with 45 million members and 17 years' worth of data had been massively undervalued. The creditors found the value to be over

$1 billion dollars. The value of Caesars customer data was higher than the value anything else including Caesars' real estate holdings, or even its brand.

Similar stories have played out around RadioShack, Sears, and Hertz. Each brand had a deep well of customers and a strong lock on the analytics behind them but could not proactively apply these valuable customer insights in time to save their brands.

Customers Empowered and Unleashed

We have entered a new business era. An era where the customers are so powerful that companies clamor to serve them. Imagine the possibilities: Airlines that send cars to pick you up before your flight and then escort you through security; shoe companies that first review your wardrobe then send matching styles in your size for you to try on; or grocery stores that stock your refrigerator with ready-made meals customized to your dietary needs while you work.

In each of these examples, a company is *almost* at the highest levels of customer centricity. AirFrance or American Airlines have been known to escort premium customers right through security, but it is not inevitable. Zappos will deliver shoes and provide excellent customer support but not send you a wardrobe consultant to evaluate your current shoe needs. And eMeals will send ready-made meal plans but not consult your refrigerator about its contents. Today's fastest-growing firms are quickly learning how to please valuable customers and along the way, deeply connecting with these customers by answering the needs of their busy lives. In a customer era, the product is secondary to the customer. As a result, customer expectations, experience, and even the values of the companies with which they will transact have come surging forward.

The Roots of the Customer Era

At 26, I sat on the board of a Silicon Valley venture-backed company that I cofounded. The highlight of every board meeting for me was when the VCs would quiz me about our customer relationships. What I did not understand then was how much those ongoing good customer relationships minimized their investment risk and maximized their potential return. Solid customer relationships are not just the sign of a good company that cares about its customers. Solid customer relationships are quantified business gold, for reasons that I will share in this book. (Also, keep in mind that "customer" throughout this book means the purchaser of your product. That could be a consumer, player, fan, or any number of customer-centric names.)

Many years later when I worked in the new field of digital analytics, I noticed a common complaint among analysts was that their recommendations were rarely taken seriously. The disconnect was palpable. The analysts were loaded down with technical digital marketing jargon and pseudo key performance indicators (KPIs) that measured the time a customer spent on a site or page views per visit. It seems like this data should have meant something, but without the connection to the boardroom, it did not.

For many years, this standoff between business-relevant, board-level information and data signals sent by customers controlled how companies did business. Then in 2006 everything began to change, and the customer era was born. Companies were finally making the connection between marketing activity and boardroom impact. What changed?

Two data megatrends collided. One was social media and the other was mobile usage.

Customer Data Megatrends

Social media was on fire in the early 2000s and started to peak right around 2007-2008. I remember this specifically because I was just married and well into my career at this time and social media initially connected with those of college age looking to meet a mate. It quickly spread to all age groups and around the world, so much so that the only demographics where it is still growing are the over 65 age crowd and Africa (which continues to bring more people online).

This social media megatrend had a huge effect on customer data. It wasn't simply that there was more data. Now the data was rich with the voice of customers advocating for products they liked and harshly reviewing the ones they did not. New digital tools sprung up around tracking brand words, competitors, and deriving public opinion from sentiment analysis. Then, the first viral videos about customer experience emerged. One powerful example was the hit song "United Breaks Guitars," which was released in 2009 and relates Dave Carroll's personal experience on a 2008 flight. Carroll watched United Airlines' baggage handlers abuse his guitar case, the guitar was delivered broken, and then United refused to cover it over a lengthy customer service saga. Not only did the video go viral and embarrass United, but in the weeks following its release, United's stock price fell 10 percent, costing shareholders $180 million dollars in value. The power of one customer's voice was quantified.[1]

The second data megatrend came from Mary Meeker's annual Internet Trends report. In 2016, for the first time, mobile device usage overtook desktops. Today you might be hard-pressed to remember what it was like to always have to go back to your computer to look something up on the internet instead of just pulling out your mobile device. Back then, stores were in a panic because so many customers were "showrooming." This meant they were coming to the stores to try out a product or get more information but then completing the purchase online where the same product could often be acquired for a lower price. The constantly connected internet mobile device was the pin that punctured the offline world with digital pricing transparency.

The impact of this transparency was—again—to increase customer power, but it also provided fresh streams of individualized data. Because people use mobile devices in the moment to research products or look up reviews, it became an ideal medium for understanding individual behavior, sometimes called *intent*. Further, mobile data is geographically contextual. That means a business owner can tell if you are standing

• • •

[1] It was widely reported that within four weeks of the video being posted online, United Airlines' stock price fell 10 percent, costing stockholders about $180 million in value. Source: via Wikipedia United Breaks Guitars page—Ayres, Chris (July 22, 2009). "Revenge is best served cold – on YouTube: How a broken guitar became a smash hit". *The Sunday Times*. Archived from the original on May 31, 2010. Retrieved July 7, 2010.

within the store, around the corner, or if you are somewhere else when you search for relevant products.

Social media and mobile devices did not just create avalanches of big data. They added behavioral context attached to a person (whether identified or analyzed anonymously as part of a larger group) that dramatically increased both customer power and simultaneously enabled the connection between marketing activity and customer equity. In other words, the era of customer centricity would not be here without social media or mobile devices.

Ten years later, customers grew concerned about how much their social media, mobile devices, and web behavior as well as personally identifiable information (PII) was being used without their control or consent. The backlash created first the European regulations (GDPR) and later the U.S. regulations (CCPA). While the precise implications remain nebulous as lawsuits proceed and tracking methods change, we know companies who want to build a base of healthy customers can rely on two things:

1. **The use of customer data must pass the "sunshine test."** In other words, if it were released as public news, it must stand up to rational scrutiny. For example, few customers would protest the desire of a company to announce new products to previous purchasers. But general consumers (not customers) could rightly protest the invasion of personal devices with text messages encouraging them to buy items based on their search behavior as they walk down the street. Consent must be clear.

2. **Customers and consumers are willing to trade data for value.** Asking for data without explaining the value to be returned is no longer acceptable. For example, most people have a phone number connected to their grocery store loyalty number which allows instant discounts at checkout. What would not be acceptable is if that grocery store sold individual purchase data to health insurance companies who then analyzed healthy eating habits and adjusted rates. The trade for value must be acceptable, approved, and permissioned by the customer before use.

In the quest for quality customers and new revenue streams, companies must not forget to pass the sunshine test and to limit the trade-for-value to its original purpose. Privacy regulations help keep this balance in place.

The Equity Connection

How should companies think about customer data and its value? On April 14th, 2015, a revolutionary article summarizing the rising power of the customer appeared in *Harvard Business Review*. The authors selected data from 6,000 different mergers and acquisitions that occurred between 2003 and 2013. Over this 10-year period of investment activity, they classified how companies were valued into brand and customer equity. Brand value is expressed through trademarks and product names while the value of customers is attached to repeat purchases. Their goal was to understand how company valuation had changed since the birth of ecommerce.

In the chart showing in Figure I-1, the light gray line shows the declining value of brands, and the dark gray line illustrates the rise of the customer value.[2] From start to finish, it's almost a 100-percent switch—the

FIGURE I-1

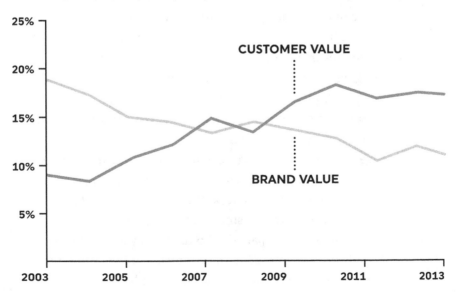

Change in Measured Company Value

customer value ends up at about 18 percent and the brand value ends up at about 11 percent. In other words, the value of a company is increasingly tied to its customers.

So, what exactly is customer equity? *Customer equity* is the total future customer lifetime value (CLV) or "unlocked potential revenue" of all your current customers. It is a statistical prediction of how much each customer will likely spend. It is unlocked because the revenue has not been received. For example, if I purchase a pair of Nike tennis shoes, then I have some statistical chance of buying products from Nike again. Every month I do not buy, that chance gets smaller and smaller but, mathematically speaking, it never goes to zero. The value of a dollar also changes over time. Adding this customer potential together provides the customer equity number and helps answer the question, "What is the value of your customer base?"

What to Expect In This Book

As an industry insider, I've had the unique privilege to see inside dozens of Fortune 500 brands as well as fast-moving, direct-to-consumer startups. Through over 100 interviews, as well as knowledge gained at C-level conferences and through conversations with industry experts, I have learned how companies move through a customer-centric transformation and the massive payoffs they see as they become unstoppable industry leaders. Simply put, a healthy company has healthy customers. The challenge is most companies cannot clearly listen or learn from their customer base and as a result, they are not industry leaders. Today's customers are constantly changing, but through the artful use of data, industry leaders keep up. I'll show you the critical turns on this journey so your company can keep up, too.

● ● ●

2 Notice the way that the two measures begin on the left and how they move over the 10-year period to the right. There's a gray line that starts at about 19 percent, and that is the line for brand value. There's another line that starts at about 9 percent and that is the line for customer value. And year over year as they move forward, they start to change. Right about 2007 to 2008 the equity lines change, and customer value starts to grow, and brand values start to decrease, then they continue to switch.

What does it mean to keep up? It means having a clear understanding of what products are resonating with individual customers and why. It means creating an internal culture that not only values the customer, but one where teams align to clear hurdles and create long-term 9- and 10-figure gains. But most of all, it means having the humility to be of service to the customer and recognize their collective strength.

In this book, I will also share a series of real stories from my podcast, *The Customer Equity Accelerator*. By hearing how real companies talk about their successes and struggles within the framework of customer-centric leadership, my hope is to give you a clear sense of reality as well as arm your strategic thinking. I have also included an assessment in Chapter 2 to help you pinpoint where your organization is, what you should be thinking about, and how to know when your company has graduated from one zone to the next. The customer-centric maturity curve is the roadmap that you can follow to get transformational results.

• • •

CUSTOMER-CENTRIC TAKEAWAYS

➔ The transformation of business from product-centric to customer-centric has been percolating since the era of direct mail and customer relationship management platforms. The difference now is the avalanche of digitally connected customer data which has been steadily growing since 2008.

➔ Quality customer data is so valuable it surpasses the value of everything else in the business including brand marks and real estate.

➔ Leading investment firms are starting to value public and private companies on the quality of their customer base.

➔ This book presents a roadmap to transform the way companies use customer data to listen, learn from, and ultimately lead innovations by knowing and serving their customers best.

CHAPTER 1

Getting To Know Customer-Centricity

MOST COMPANIES believe they are customer-centric because they truly care about their customers. They work hard to deliver meaningful customer experiences and high satisfaction. This is a wonderful starting point, but it is a bit like saying you are a Colorado native because you spent a little time skiing there. Being truly customer-centric is an infectious culture, a way of life that takes over your company from the boardroom to the war room and does not stop. It is a long-term initiative that becomes a permanent way of working.

In this chapter, you will learn the foundational concepts of customer-centric thinking, and you'll meet some people who know the topic well. At the end, you should understand the connection between customer equity and customer lifetime value, how companies can now be valued based on the quality of their customers, and why customer-centric thinking is not the same as product-centric thinking.

Let's start with why it is important to see good customers—specifically not all customers—as an asset, as illustrated in my next interview with private equity investor, **Anthony Choe.**

Maximizing CLV with Anthony Choe, Founder of Provenance

There is no such thing as an average customer. While it's easy to say the customer is the most important asset of a business, few have spent time quantifying what that truly means. Anthony Choe is one of those few. As the founder of Provenance, a progressive consumer private equity firm, Anthony uses customer lifetime value (CLV), which you read about in the introduction, as the primary lens for evaluating businesses. He explains how predictive CLV provides precision and allows both the investor and company to have a singular focus on the customer among all the data noise. With the increasing availability of data and marketing tools, he believes CLV principles are timeless. Optimizing around CLV will always be the best answer, regardless of channel, regardless of the marketing message, regardless of shifting landscapes. As I spoke with Anthony about how he views CLV, I really wanted to understand not only the CLV connection but what companies could do to maximize it.

Here is a look at our conversation.

Tell us a little bit about your background and how you were drawn to this topic around customer equity. It's not something we usually walk around talking about.

Choe: When I first started working, I got into investment banking in the mid-nineties at a place called DLJ, and it was a fantastic environment. It was the hotbed for financing for private equity firms, back when they were called "buyout shops." And so, I kind of caught the bug for private equity there and while I was at DLJ I got a call from Brentwood Associates, which was an LA-based private equity firm that had its heritage originally as a venture capital firm. So, I was excited. I joined them in '96, and at that point, it wasn't really a consumer-focused firm, but by hook or crook, we began focusing more and more on consumers and by 2001 we decided to focus exclusively on the consumer.

It was a really good time to do that. And you know, back then there was a lot of change that was happening in the industry. It wasn't that everybody was talking about Amazon. Everybody was talking about Walmart, believe it or not, how Walmart was going to be the dominant retailer on the planet. So, it's kind of ironic now that the roles have reversed a little bit. Now it's Amazon that everybody's worried about. But Amazon was on the rise at that point, and it was also clear by 2000, once we were coming off the bursting of the dotcom bubble, that ecommerce was here to stay, and it was changing how brands could interact with consumers. In many ways, it was the most democratizing event in the history of brands that we've ever seen. So, by 2005, we became the first private equity investor to focus on brands selling direct-to-consumer in a multichannel fashion. And it wasn't really, well, understood what the heck all that "omnichannel" stuff meant. I wrote a 120-page white paper for our investors explaining why this was a permanent shift in the landscape.

This reminds me of Jerry Maguire. *Did you run in, (and I have this picture in my head based on the movie) with your manuscript, and everybody stops and looks at you, and you said, "No, we've got to focus on the customer"?*
Choe: Yeah. It was actually a little bit like that. I wouldn't say there was one singular "aha" moment, but there were a series of "aha" moments between 2000 and 2005 where it all kind of became obvious. So, I guess it's obvious in hindsight, but it wasn't obvious at the time. But yeah, we were fortunate enough to have some specialty retail investments and some catalog investments that gave us some visibility as to what was going on in ecommerce. It was very clear that ecommerce was going be the unifying channel that was going to tie all the other channels together, but also that it would eventually become the primary channel by which brands would get launched. At Provenance, we're pretty currently into that stage of the game. I can't say I started my career with some grand vision to do consumer private equity, but I was very, very fortunate that all those fortunate

happenstances started us on the path to hone our understanding of customer lifetime value.

Can you say a bit more about how you use that today, and why Provenance is perhaps a little different than other private equity firms?
Choe: So, what's different about the consumer now, at least from what I've seen, is that because brands are starting their lives digitally first, in many ways, the shape of the growth curve is different. So, in the old days when you were starting a catalog, or a specialty retailer, or whatever the case might be, you have to slog it out for a good 10 years. Sometimes as an entrepreneur, not really having much capital available, bootstrapping yourself to eventually kind of prove that you had a brand and then you could start to step on the accelerator a little bit. With ecommerce as the first channel that most brands are really starting with, the shape of the growth is different. You can come out of the blocks screaming with a very high growth rate, being relatively efficient. You can outsource a lot of the key functions of the company early on and eventually bring them in-house over time.

Growth is happening faster earlier, which is why I think it's become an interesting area to invest in because there is the potential for attractive growth.

By the time we're investing money, $15 million of primary capital is typically enough. I think for brands if you raise too much money, it is actually going to be difficult to have an attractive exit. So that puts a really high imperative on brands to grow fast enough to hit the market opportunity and the brand resonance while it's there, but also be highly efficient along the way. And that's where I think customer lifetime value principles become extraordinarily important to be precise so that you're not wasting capital.

Why should I care about my customers as an asset and how does that connect into customer lifetime value?
Choe: So ultimately, I think this is all about precision for me as an investor and precision for the company, then making its optimization decisions. But what you have in direct-to-consumer

business is an explosion of data that's available because when you're selling to individual customers, you're sitting on a treasure trove of data. So when we were designing ourselves, we wanted to be able to do that from the ground up. If you're a student of long-term fundamental investing, going all the way back to Benjamin Graham, sound investment decisions are always a function of value that you're investing in relative to the asset that you're buying.

Consumer brands though, you hear everybody talk about in general terms, but never with any specificity that the customer is the most important asset in the business. And we all know that, but nobody has really spent time quantifying what that means. But now with the help of predictive CLV techniques, we can literally define the shape of the customer asset depreciation curve. And to me, that's a pretty profound insight that nobody is taking advantage of. If you have a heavy asset business—and the customer is very asset heavy, consumer brands are very asset heavy in the customer—well, if you're doing that, you should have a pretty good idea of what it is. That is the asset that you're actually buying.

That's incredibly important. I just really want to underscore that because not only are we defining what the value of the customer asset is, but what you said that is so interesting is it's predictive CLV, and you're about looking at a depreciation curve. In other words, I'm not always assuming that my customers are going to perform at the same level just because they bought once, or that my high-value customers are going to continue being my high-value customers. So, the fact that there are some dynamics built in that it's flexing and flowing is an incredibly important concept, and we can model that.
Choe: Exactly. I mean, what if you're a car rental company or an oil and gas company drilling a well, you have these assets, and you probably know what their useful lives are, and you probably know how much value you're likely to extract out of it over a given period. That all seems very fundamental and natural. How could you look at these businesses in any other way? Well, guess what, the customer asset is the same, and now we have the tools to be able to quantify

it. So that's what we're super excited about from the investing perspective. But equally, these insights are always only as good as the implementation of what happens in real life once you invest.

We're helping companies see their businesses in ways that they had never seen before. When you have the opportunity to impact how companies are optimizing their decision making with a very efficient process, that's what's most impactful to us. In private equity, you're not able to trade in and out of investments like you can in the public market. You're really making long-term bets and being able to move the needle on some of the operating decisions. How you're doing stuff more efficiently in the business is where the rubber really starts to meet the road.

When you help these companies, what kinds of things are you helping them think through?
Choe: It's actually hard to think of areas where customer lifetime value as the primary lens *doesn't* help you impact the business. Marketing is certainly one, but believe it or not, retail site selection, if you know how to apply certain tools also becomes very lifetime value driven. Merchandising decisions, ad creative, how you're optimizing those areas. Everything can be looked at through this lens, and it's the right lens to look at everything through in the long run. So, giving you a concrete example, certainly on the marketing side, we recently invested in a custom menswear business based in New York called Knot Standard. And while the company is on the small side for us, we saw that it built an exceptionally loyal customer base with customer repeat rates uncommon for an apparel brand. So the result of this is that they have super-high customer lifetime value measured in the several thousands, not several hundreds per customer.

When you look at the marketing spend for a product with very attractive gross margins, the ROI was closer to 10 times on that marketing dollar than two times, which is more typical of what we see. So that's a case where we said it wasn't because their marketing is so sophisticated. What it means is they're actually under-investing in marketing. They should be doing more, they could be doing more, and it's screaming for more capital to apply to that effort because the ROI is so high. So that's one easy way that we see it from a marketing and investment perspective. It is a contrast with certain other businesses that are highly transactional in nature, which often we see in the home category. Let's say certain furniture businesses are pretty high-ticket, and you may not see a customer repeat purchase over a long period of time. So, when you're looking at customer lifetime value, that lifetime is basically the first transaction.

We've seen lots of companies with high average order values (AOVs) and good margins scale to $50 million dollars with very little outside capital, and that is a big accomplishment. I don't want to downplay that, growing a business to $50 million in three or four years with no outside capital, that's a pretty impressive feat. But for us, when we look at it, we say, "Well, the company is forever going to be on a customer acquisition treadmill because there's no downstream customer spend. And the customer assets are a very leaky bucket." While it's impressive, it's not necessarily the right fit for us.

For customer assets there's a fundamental assumption in the first example you gave about Knot Standard that I can get more and more loyal customers. It's almost like the initial customers that came in are really good and there's an assumption that there are hundreds, thousands, maybe millions more just like them. Is that indeed true? Or in either case, are you still always on an acquisition treadmill?
Choe: Yeah, well there's always going to be a wide variety of customers that you're going to be attracting. Some are always going to be a higher value than others. What's important for our purposes is to have a deep understanding of who it is those loyal customers are, what they look like, what they'd behave like demographically, psychographically. You can be more efficient about hunting for more of them in the future. It's a little bit like you're going to have to cast that net and when you're fishing, and you know you'd like to catch nothing but whales, but there will be a lot of minnows in there that get caught up as a byproduct, but you're still casting a net. There's

always going to be heterogeneity in the variety of customers that you get. So, I think what we've seen in our conversations with the companies that we've talked to is we're saying there is no such thing as an average customer is it's kind of an enlightening thing for the company.

So, ecommerce companies are typically very good at doing some basic level of cohort analysis, so tracking a group of customers that were acquired in a certain quarter in a certain year and tracking their behavior over time, but time is only one dimension that you need to look at the data over. Most people haven't looked at the spread of what comprises the average, and so people are actually surprised when we show them that typically 20 percent of customers are creating 65 percent of the value and the average is really comprised of a barbell. You have a lot of one-time customers who were interested in what you're doing; they've made a purchase. They may never make a purchase again, and that's probably the majority of your customer base. On the other end, you've got a tail of customers who absolutely love what you're doing, buy from you time and time again, tell all their friends about what you're doing, and they're super high value.

The average sits in between the two ends of the barbell, and so when you're optimizing your business, and you're using average customer metrics, you're actually optimizing to where almost none of your customers are—or at least where none of the value is. So, you have to be able to make money on some of the lower value customers. You're not trying to fire all of them, but you're trying to minimize the losses or maximize whatever little gains you're making out of those customers while at the same time really taking care of the super loyalists and making sure that they continue to buy from you at a high rate because they're the ones that are really buttering the bread in the long run.

I think a lot of people understand the value of loyal customers over time. That makes sense, but I think where people tend to lose perspective is the fact that those loyal customers have a specific profile. As you dig into more about why they're doing what they do, then you can adjust your products and services and even your retail location around that group. There's another side to this principle, which is that you can't take a low-value customer and grow them into a high-value customer, and I've heard a lot of contradiction on this. Some people believe you can. Some people believe you can't. What is your opinion?

Choe: Well, I think you can, but you just have to be efficient with the resources that you're willing to spend to try to test to see if you can do it. I don't think you shouldn't try, but I don't think you can afford to bend over backward to try to make somebody into something they're not. There is a lot of incremental value that we see to doing retention marketing and using certain principles to welcome all of your initial customers into the brand to try to stimulate their interest and demand over time. The key is not to spend too much to try to entice that next purchase. Whether it's severe discounting or overcommunicating, certain customers are never going to convert to that second purchase. You can't try too hard or apply too many resources or do too much discounting.

I love that point about severe discounting. When you're considering the value of the performance of customers as an asset, you have to push liabilities, and discounting them becomes a liability that weighs down the performance of that asset. I could see where severe discounting, in addition to being not a great tool to acquire really good long-term customers, is actually weighing down the performance of your company.

Choe: Absolutely. We see a lot of mistakes being made around what the average customer looks like. We typically see companies do some amount of survey work or demographic, psychographic work to try to get a picture of what the "average" customer is. And going back to our conversation earlier, our view at Provenance is that the marketplace for any given vertical or category is going to be a lot more fragmented over time. And what we're seeing is that the fragmentation is happening around certain "tribes," for lack of a better word, and you have to be pretty precise about who your tribe is. And the mistake that we see a lot of companies making is they either falsely believe that a majority of their customers are of [one category of customers, when measured by customer *count*. But it's not necessarily true that the majority of *value creation* is coming from this category].

I won't name any names, but we looked at a company where they were firmly convinced that 55 percent of their customers were Millennials. When we applied customer lifetime value to each customer, it was clear that a majority of the value creation was actually coming from Gen X and Baby Boomers. And you know, they kind of had this sunken expression on their face, and they were kind of bummed out. They thought they weren't as cool as they thought they were, but I told them "Guys, don't be disappointed by this. You should be ecstatic because you have a three-generation span of appeal as a brand and you're highly relevant to Millennials, but just give them time because they haven't entered the sweet spot of their earnings or wealth curve like Gen Xers, and Boomers have, so they can't afford to be more loyal to you than they currently are, but they love what you're doing. The good news is that your brand has a future, because it's highly relevant to the next generation of high-disposable incomes. The value doesn't all have to be coming from Millennials today."

What a great way to think about the business. I want to circle back to what you said a minute ago about tribes, understanding the right tribe, and how tribe is different than what we might think of as the Gen X-er persona or the other types of personas.
Choe: Here's where things have to get a lot more specific today. I think it has a lot more to do with psychographics than it does with demographics. If you look at niche brands and, in particular, direct-to-consumer brands, this is something that I've seen for 15 years that's true: All of them are targeting consumers in the top 20-25 percent of the income brackets regardless of age. That's not perfectly true, but in a vast majority of instances, that's true. It's already a self-selected universe of people that you're targeting. Age and income aren't really helping you be more specific. So, it really comes down to psychographics. What are the predilections of people's choices

that have nothing to do with age or income, sort of your beliefs, your philosophies, your attitudes?

And that's where it feels like the brand selection is happening a lot more by tribe because people are differentiating that way much more so than they used to. It's almost like the criteria for selecting brands aren't around, "Well, is this a good price-value equation for me?" because, at this point, the competitive bar is so high for price-value that if you don't have a good price-value proposition, you're not even in the game. You're not going to be around long enough to even think about these questions.

How people are choosing their brands has more to do with what they think fits their personality profile more so than, "Hey, is this a better sneaker for the dollar than the other brand that I could consider?" It's almost like the brand [selection process] is a reflection of how you would pick your friends.

How would I take the next steps to improve my customer equity?
Choe: Once you get used to some of these principles, my personal opinion is that every company should be able to do some of the analytics internally themselves. Whether it's cohort tracking, value-based segmentation, and even if you're doing it on a historical basis and not a predictive one, I feel like a company should always be experimenting with the data that they're sitting on and being able to manipulate some stuff yourself is always a good thing.

I'm going to echo what you said there because the company has to have a perspective. They have to have strategic leadership behind the data, so it's not enough just to say, "I have this value in the customer base." You have to have this sense of how you go to market with that customer base. How do you make choices about what's important, where do you want to spend, and what do you want to do across the board? Instead, a lot of companies don't have that strong perspective. They leave it to the tactical folks to figure out, so I just want to underscore your point about the need for leadership to own the analytics, run some of it internally, and understand it to get that comprehensive strategy together.

Choe: What I love about CLV principles is that they're timeless. The amount of data that's going to be available to people is going to be constantly increasing. There are always going to be new marketing methods, but regardless of all those environmental changes that are happening, optimizing around CLV is always going to be the best answer regardless of the channel marketing message.

Anthony's interview underscores the connection between the value of a company and the value of a high-quality customer base, the customer equity you read about earlier. He gives the start-ups he works with a competitive edge by knowing exactly where their products and marketing messages resonate and further tracking this trend via CLV over time. When customer data is pinned together correctly, it forms a powerful advantage that supports the sustainability of a company. In my next interview with Dan McCarthy, we discuss exactly how the customer equity connection can create an impact—even jarring Wall Street's big investment firms.

Using Data to Synthesize Marketing and Finance with Dan McCarthy, Assistant Professor of Marketing at Emory University

Not every dollar is created equally. **Dan McCarthy**, Assistant Professor of Marketing at Emory University, talks about customer-based corporate valuation (CBCV), which is an innovative approach to evaluating the current and future financial health of a company based on its customer metrics. He shares how CBCV synthesizes marketing and finance together, allowing marketers to speak the CFO's language about the potential value being driven for the company and its impact. As I spoke with Dan, I wanted him to explain how the model forces a focus on customers as the metric of measurement for future revenue, solves the measurement problem of what's happening currently, and allows for more accurate predictive valuation. Here's a look at our conversation.

Dan, what is your background and how were you drawn to this topic?
McCarthy: I went to the Wharton School for undergraduate, and
I concentrated in finance and statistics as well as system science
engineering. Back in 2006 when I graduated, what everyone did
was go to Wall Street. I went to a hedge fund. I was there for a
number of years before coming back. My true passion was applying
quantitative models. I went back to Wharton for my Ph.D. in
statistics. And I'd say the wonderful thing about customer base
corporate valuation is really—which why it ended up very quickly
becoming the centerpiece of my Ph.D. dissertation—is that it really
brings together all three of those worlds. We're essentially thinking
about the overall valuation of firms, but it's also very heavily
statistics and marketing because we need quantitative models that
are fairly sophisticated to be able to make the accurate predictions
that we need to perform valuation accurately. And obviously what
we're predicting is the behavior of customers, which is the world of
marketing models. It's really been a true pleasure, and it's been just
super exciting to see the level of enthusiasm that we've received
about this work.

If you were to describe customer-based corporate valuation that is a
little bit more for the layperson, how would you describe it?
McCarthy: It's actually fairly simple. Essentially when you're doing
valuation of the company, one of the big things you need to do is
predict what that company's future revenues are going to be. For
customer-based businesses that derive most of the revenue from
customers, for every dollar of revenues that the company generates,
there has to be a customer who's making a purchase. To the extent
that we can predict the flow of customers being acquired over time,
the number of purchases they are going to make, and how much
they're going to spend on those purchases, that has to give us the
revenues of the company. So essentially there's nothing really new
here in the sense that all we're doing is really making an enlightened
revenue projection. The key is how we get there.

When you say the key is how you get there, I imagine you're saying that you might be standing on the shoulders of previous models, but now we're using a more precise or more accurate model. Would that be fair?
McCarthy: Yeah, in some sense it's standing on the shoulders of marketing giants. We've got these great models that have been studied and analyzed and improved on within marketing. And one of the big innovations is to take those great marketing models and bring them into the world of finance. Within finance we run the customer-based marketing models and use those to come up with our revenue projections instead of doing it the traditional way. The traditional way is to say revenues grew 55 percent last year and the year before, so I think it's going to grow another three percent this year, which is just not as accurate. How you arrive at the projection is almost as important as the projection itself.

For example, you can have a dollar of revenue come in and to the same degree that not all customers are created equal, not all revenue dollars are created equal. If I'm getting that revenue dollar from a customer who I know is going to keep coming back for the next five years, that dollar is going to mean a lot more. I pay a lot more for it than a revenue dollar from the customer that has very low retention. So, it's just a lot of nuance and detail that we get from thinking about things from the vantage point of the customer that we just completely lose when we go to that traditional way of thinking within finance.

Can you walk us through the different people who should care about customer-based corporate valuation and why they should care?
McCarthy: It's an extremely important question. So first, there's the marketing department. You have people like you and me, and if I'm a marketing manager, I need a marketing budget. The tough part is if I go to the CFO and tell him or her, I need this marketing budget so I can improve the customer experience or change the customer journey, I'm sure the CFO will appreciate that on some level, but CFOs are very dollars and cents focused. With this work, we change the conversation to one that is essentially the same language that the CFO is speaking. So, you'd be able to say with this marketing

budget, "I will be able to expand the value of the business by x," and that's something the CFO could very much get on board with.

The flip side of the coin are the people in finance. They're the people who actually are buying the stock or selling stock on a day-to-day basis and, ultimately, they're the ones who will determine what the valuation of your firm will be. This is extremely important to them because essentially it represents a whole new dimension of the valuation equation. This is an important source of signal for them to make potentially more profitable investment decisions. Within finance, it can also be really useful for private equity firms because, in addition to being able to come up with some projection of what the value of the firm should be, they can think about some of the marketing levers they can pull to improve customer retention or improve the efficiency of their new customer acquisition spend to further enhance the value of the company.

Is customer-based corporate valuation really here to stay or is it a passing fad?
McCarthy: It's here to stay. I think that saying that customer-based corporate valuation is a fad would be like saying discounted cashflow (DCF) valuation is a fad. DCF valuation is the de facto standard way of valuating firms. Just purely by accounting, this has to be true. This is a model for how customers behave, rolling that up and using that to come up with an accurate revenue forecast that decomposition cannot be false. So as long as we have the data, this will be valuable, and it will be very diagnostic. I really do think we're in the first innings of this.

Each time we've done an example, say Blue Apron or Wayfair, we've seen a dramatic reaction from the financial community or from the popular media. I'd say we're finally getting to the point where we see real adoption by people other than us.

Let's talk about the Blue Apron and the Wayfair examples that you mentioned and get a little more specific about the models that you use inside the concept of customer-based corporate valuation.

McCarthy: Blue Apron put out an IPO prospectus, which is what all companies do before they go public.

I took a look [at Blue Apron's prospectus], and the first thing that was very surprising was they didn't disclose anything about customer retention or customer churn even though they're fundamentally a subscription-based business, and a lot of their peers do disclose those sorts of metrics. So that was interesting. But they did disclose some data points about their customers. Essentially the picture that they were painting was one of everything going up into the right, and so they were saying, "Our revenues are growing strongly. Our active customer accounts growing strongly, look at our order growth." Even though I couldn't apply the exact methodology from a paper I had co-written with Pete Fader on subscription-based evaluation, I applied a very similar model, and it allowed me to uncover what the company's retention curve actually was even though they didn't disclose it.

And the punchline was, they acquire 100 customers but roll forward the clock by six months and about 70 percent of those customers will have churned. And that is far worse than companies like Netflix or Dollar Shave Club that retain almost twice as many customers. I posted it to LinkedIn and that piece ended up going viral. So, it ended up in *The Wall Street Journal* multiple times, *Fortune, Forbes, Barron's*, you name it. The rest of the story for them is history. Originally, they had priced the IPO at $15 to $17 per share. About five days after I released the detailed analysis, they cut the price range to the $10 to $11 a share. They IPO'd at 10 and now that they're sitting below $3 a share.

I really do feel like it was a very good example of we had this one image that was being painted, which is traditional venture capital growth at all costs. We're just going to eventually grow ourselves into profitability. Don't worry about the fact that we're losing money right now. On the flip side, you dip beneath the surface and see actually the fundamentals at the customer level are eroding and are really not looking good.

Do you think if the companies that took them public had they done this kind of model valuation, would they have ever gotten out of the IPO gate?
McCarthy: I think that the people who pushed them in this direction was the VC community. I think that there are many companies including some other subscription box companies who have folded up shop who essentially said, "We pursued this growth-at-all-costs model." It was promoted by the venture capital firms that essentially just gave them a lot of money and said, "Grow!" I think that model is becoming less and less relevant. There is a pocket of people within VC community like Anthony Choe within private equity that are waking up to the importance of revenue stability, not just revenue growth and the importance of unit economics. That strategy itself is destroying value. To the extent that we can prevent companies from doing that, it's just going to retain the value that otherwise would have been destroyed.

Let's shift gears to your second example, Wayfair. How did that one shape up and what did you learn in those models?
McCarthy: [Wayfair] was a fundamentally different story. We had put out the original paper on how we can do valuation for subscription businesses, and now we were doing the same thing for non-subscription. We searched around and found Overstock and Wayfair. They were two companies that just so happened to disclose a pretty good amount of customer data in their public filings. So, we repeated the analysis for them and essentially the conclusion that we reached was that Overstock evaluation seem fairly reasonable. We ran a related model where we predicted how many customers we're going acquire in the future, the cost that we will incur to acquire each of those customers, the flow of subsequent purchases that those customers make until they churn, and then a model for basket size. The resulting revenue forecast led to a valuation that was close to Overstock's then-current stock price. But when we ran the exact same model for Wayfair, we came to a very different conclusion. We inferred that their stock should be worth something like one-sixth what it had been trading.

We were very struck by that, and we did not want that to be the conclusion. But it was what our model implied, so we had just to be scientists, and that's what we had to report. So, we did. That ended up in *The Wall Street Journal*. We ended up on a conference call with about 70 hedge funds moderated by the sell-side firm. We were getting the calls because the day those tweets came out, the stock fell by about 10 percent. And so that ended up being the biggest one-day drop the stock had in about a year and a half. The people, I think, were thinking, "Whoa, I need to understand what this paper is saying because clearly, it's moving the market." I was getting calls from the second-largest shareholder of Wayfair and obviously they have a vested interest in saying the analysis is incorrect. And so, when money's on the line, people will do whatever it takes to essentially protect their position, and I think that's exactly what happened on both sides.

With Wayfair, you mentioned that the stock price didn't align, but was it about retention? Or acquisition?

McCarthy: It was primarily a case of customer acquisition cost. So, they were acquiring a ton of customers. I inferred that they will eventually penetrate a very substantial proportion of all U.S. households. There wasn't an issue with the volume of future acquisitions, either. And in fact, compared to Overstock, after a customer is acquired, Wayfair customers were substantially more valuable. The net present value of all the future profits that a Wayfair customer will generate after acquisition was something like 30 percent higher. The problem was Wayfair was spending way more to acquire its customers, about $69 per customer, whereas at Overstock, it was dramatically lower than that. And I inferred that at Overstock they earned about $10 for every customer they acquire.

Wayfair is losing about $10 for every customer that they acquire. In some sense then, the more customers they acquire, the less valuable they get because every customer they acquire is destroying value. It's an interesting case study. Overstock was taking the "we're not going to grow as quickly" approach. We're not going to penetrate nearly as much of the market. We are going to be stingier about how we acquire customers, even though those customers won't end up being as valuable as Wayfair customers that stinginess on the acquisition side will at least leave us with a sustainable but smaller business. So, I think again, all those components matter a lot.

What about companies that are not just B2B and B2C, but B2B2C?
McCarthy: Things get harder if you go to the example of a CPG (consumer packaged goods) company like Procter & Gamble. They don't necessarily have direct visibility to the end customer. And the same would be true, historically speaking, of a company like Nike. Historically Nike was a brand, so they sold very heavily through middlemen, whether it's Foot Locker or what have you. They've made a big pivot toward selling directly to the consumer, whether it's through their website or through their Nike stores. So suddenly now that they've made that change, they actually had the ability to observe the end customer, and that makes the modeling much easier for people like us. It's not to say that a company like Procter & Gamble to the extent that they don't have any direct-to-consumer business, can't do analysis, but it becomes much harder. And so, they may need to rely very heavily on data providers like a Nielsen and IRI using panels as opposed to the actual transaction logs.

Is there a side of the equation that's more important to address? Is it more important to address retention versus acquisition or does it just depend on the company itself?
McCarthy: It depends on the company once you've run the model yourself and you have a chance to internalize what it means for your firm. And so again, going back to the example of Blue Apron, that work really highlighted the difficulty of customer retention and secondarily the importance of customer acquisition costs, which had been moving up really concertedly before the IPO. To the extent that you want to put the pressure where the pain is, maybe they should be spending a lot of time thinking about how they can improve the

retention profile of their customers and/or make their customer acquisition spending more efficient. If it were a different company that sells product at a loss, it could be that they had no issues with customer acquisition cost. It could be that they need to really think about targeted cost reductions.

I think it really does kind of depend on the context, but what will remain constant in all of those examples is the overarching value framework that's going to remain the same. We can be able to think about the value of your firm by thinking about the quantity and quality of the customers you will acquire in the future, retention of all of your customers, whether they're existing or future, your ability to get orders out of those customers, the amount that they spend on those orders, and the cost to serve the customer. That framework will always be the same.

That's back to the core challenge that it is the customer that drives your business, especially in the marketing world where we're often distracted by channels. I often say that channels don't buy products. Customers buy products. You have to get to customers.
McCarthy: We hear the same thing with products: "We need to sell this product." No. What you need to do is build a portfolio of products or a portfolio of channels that are synchronized and expand the value for the customer, but ultimately, it's CLV that matters the most.

First, I have to understand what's happening. Second, within those measurements, I need to look at the specific focus that's right for my business. You can't just pick up what happened at Wayfair, what happened at Blue Apron and blanket apply it. You have to really understand your business concerning the model, and that's where your internal subject matter experts become incredibly important for deciding the right way to move forward.
McCarthy: If I were to build up this a little bit based on what you just mentioned, there's [the question of], "What's happening to my firm?" Then, "What's happening to me relative to my competition to establish a baseline level of what good performance actually is?"

And then the third would be, "What's my performance relative to my performance in the past?" And so even if you are, say, Netflix, which has done a wonderful job of creating very high CLV customers and acquiring a lot of them over time, they can essentially run models like these every month or every single quarter and be able to say how much CLV they did acquire and what was the average CLV per acquired customer. Is that trending up or down? And that could be a way to help push good companies to become even better. So, this is not just a methodology for flagging companies looking to turn themselves around. This is something that is applicable to virtually all customer-driven businesses.

I almost think that there are a limited number of good customers out there, and the companies who do this now will have a substantial competitive advantage. Do you think that's a correct assumption?
McCarthy: Yeah. Better to come out in front of it then to continue with the status quo, but then get bushwhacked two years from now.

Dan's interview helps us understand that when a company deeply grasps the diverse behavior of its customer base and can attach that to C-suite financials, they can very quickly find and fix acquisition, retention, and other problems before it's too late. These are the fundamentals that make a company financially sustainable. A few companies such as Spotify, Slack, Dropbox, Lyft, The RealReal, and Farfetch proudly report their customer cohort chart on public investor calls now. Whether you choose to report these metrics now or later, it is high time to diagnose your business by tuning into your customer base.

Almost every business I have spoken to says they are customer-centric, even if they are not. Why is this so? First, there is a cultural implication behind this question that implies the business does not care about its customers. Not so. Every business cares about its customers. Second, this can be difficult to see. There is simply not an established way to hear the customer within the flow of financial and product data. Before we get into our last interview, let's dig into what it actually means to be customer-centric.

Customer-Centric vs. Product-Centric

For most companies, it is easier to understand "products purchased by people" than "the right customers for this product." In fact, you might even read that twice and think it is a tautology. It is not. The way we frame strategies, measure data, and build organizational structures and processes are strikingly different between a customer-centric organization and a product-centric one. According to Jay R. Galbraith who wrote *Designing the Customer-Centric Organization: A Guide to Strategy, Structure, and Process* (Jossey-Bass, 2005), the key points look like this:

FIGURE 1–1

Product Centric vs. Customer Centric

STRATEGY	**Product-Centric Company**	**Customer-Centric Company**
	Most "advanced" customer	Most profitable, loyal customer

MEASURES	**Product-Centric Company**	**Customer-Centric Company**
	Number of new products	Share of most valueable customers
	Percent of revenue from products less than two years old	Customer satisfaction
		Lifetime value of a customer
	Market share	Customer retention

Galbraith (2005) · **Designing the Customer-Centric Organization**

The measures are clearly different, but they also reflect short-term versus long-term thinking. Short-term thinking in this case is counting the number of products sold each quarter, but long-term thinking asks who is buying that product and whether their lifetime value is increasing. Short-term thinking is subject to tactics that goose the sales numbers (like massive year-end sales) to clear inventory. Long-term thinking seeks to satisfy more customer needs through innovation, reflected in the numbers as retention. In the next interview, I spoke with Jaime Colmenares, formerly the director of Americas Customer Strategy & Analytics at eBay, about this chart and the difference between customer-centric and product-centric thinking.

Customer-Centric vs. Product-Centric Thinking with Jaime Colmenares, Former Director of Americas Customer Strategy & Analytics at eBay

Most companies understand that they need to be customer-centric, but they still operate in a very product-centric way. **Jaime Colmenares** is the former director of Americas Customer Strategy & Analytics at eBay, which heads up eBay's customer analytics team that cuts across silos to better understand buyers and sellers and use the knowledge to improve business performance. Colmenares shares how being part of the finance department impacts his ability to get and use information. And he explains the different layers of data that eBay uses to bring numbers to life, including how high-CLV customers behave versus low ones, and attribution models.

As I spoke with Jaime, I wanted to know how he determined a product versus customer mindset and how he felt customer-centric companies behave. Here is a look at our conversation.

Most people think about eBay as a very product-centric company, versus a customer-centric company. Jaime, tell me a little bit more about your background and how you ended up in analytics.
Colmenares: I did my MBA at the University of California, Berkeley. After that, I spent two years as a management consultant at Bain & Company. Post Bain & Company, I wanted to continue doing the kind of work I did at Bain, and so I landed at eBay's Strategy team, spent two years there, and then transitioned into analytics also here at eBay. I've spent the past four years here now.

I always think it's interesting that people who end up in analytics rarely start in analytics.
Colmenares: Well, it certainly was true in my case, and I transitioned into analytics precisely because of my interest in corporate strategy. It is kind of a cliche and kind of a fact that is spoken about often, that as there are more mobile phones and there are more devices out

there that are connected to the internet, more data is captured about individuals and their behavior, so analytics becomes increasingly important. I joined analytics because I eventually wanted to become an executive that was fluent in how to use data and how to translate that data into a more effective corporate strategy.

A lot of people think about eBay as a very product-centric company. I don't even know what the total volume is. It must be in the millions.
Colmenares: It's huge. We have close to a billion listings the last I heard.

What is the difference between a product-centric company versus a customer-centric company?
Colmenares: This is an important topic, and it's one that most people in business don't really quite understand. It applies to the mom-and-pop store on the corner as well as applying to your largest of the Fortune 500 companies. Most companies have the intuition that is important to understand their customers. But customer centricity is much more than just putting a line in the mission statement that says, "We're here for customers," or "Customers are first." So if I were to summarize product centricity versus customer centricity, I would say that product-centric companies focus primarily on the product or service that they produce, so they know their products very well and they know the process, the value chain to produce that product. Product-centric companies will typically know and understand their competitors as it relates to substitutes of those products, but in the product-centric view, these companies rarely make a distinction between good customers and bad customers. It doesn't matter to them who is buying the product as long as they're selling more product.

A customer-centric company on the other hand, deeply understands who that company's best customers are, and who that company's worst customers are. By "best and worst," I really mean who the most valuable customers are and who the least valuable customers are. This is important because then it gives the company a ton of insights as to who they should be serving and how they should be allocating their scarce resources. That's a quick definition of product centricity versus customer centricity.

I love the table that comes from Jay Galbraith's book. In it, he actually calls out specific differences between being product-centric and customer-centric. He basically says what you just said: With the product-centric company, you're looking for your most advanced customer regarding how many products they're buying and then in the customer-centric company, you're looking for your most profitable or your most loyal customer, which is a longer-term view. And then he goes on to outline different measures. In the product-centric company, he says people are looking at the number of new products, the percentage of revenue from products, the number of products less than two years old, and the amount of market share. A customer-centric company is looking at the share of most valuable customers, customer satisfaction, or the lifetime value of a customer and customer retention as well. Those metrics are wholly different.

Colmenares: Completely different. I see it in practice in the companies I've worked at, the companies I've consulted for, and with my colleagues in similar roles at different companies.

Is there a quick test that somebody can take to find out if they are customer-centric or product-centric?

Colmenares: Absolutely. I like to ask people a few questions. You can ask somebody, "What business are you in?" or "What does your business do?" and your listeners should go through the exercise of thinking through this for a few seconds. Their response says a lot about the center of gravity of their business. It says a lot about how that company thinks of itself. Most people will say something along the lines of, "My company produces widgets, and these widgets are better than competitors' because of x, y, or z features." But interestingly, that answer reveals how product-centric they are, and it reveals how little thought is given to customers because you'll notice that there's no mention of customers in that response.

And then another similar quick test is if you ask somebody to tell you about their customers (when companies do have some data on their customers), people will typically default to giving you answers on the "customer" or the "average customer." So, they'll say, "Our average customer spends $1,500 every 12 months, and that person buys 27 products a year." But that also reveals that even in the case of the company that has some data, they are reverting to the default of thinking about the average customer, but the average is actually very misleading. In most companies, the 80/20 rule is alive and well and so what you'll find is that most of the value and most of the sales and profits a company has are generated by a small fraction of their buyers. You can imagine that the average statistic is understating the value of your best customers and significantly overstating the value of your least valuable customers.

It seems that the first step in becoming customer centric also aligns with why you should care. You should care about being product-centric versus customer-centric.
Colmenares: Of course, of course. You should care about this if you're interested in growing profits as much as you can and for as long as you can, which essentially is every single company.

Who wouldn't be interested in that, right?
Colmenares: Exactly. Now, some companies might say that the responsibilities of the business go beyond just generating profits and those views are legitimate, but my response would be that you won't be able to do those other things with the other stakeholders, the community, for example, if you're generating losses for some considerable amount of time. Generating profits is what makes a company sustainable. It is important to clarify that the product-centric model has worked for some time for many companies and will probably continue to work for some companies for a long time. But what you'll find is that as competitive pressure is intensifying between companies and as investors are becoming more demanding, those companies that can provide a valuable service to their customers will outperform.

I always think that product-centric model is people who have a lot of scale and a corner on the market, they are the sole supplier or one of the few suppliers of a product, or maybe they just have better pricing than anyone else. To me, that always smells like being product-centric.

Colmenares: Absolutely. Michael Porter says that essentially there are two ways to compete: with cost leadership or with product differentiation. In the cost leadership world, it's all about economies of scale. If you have larger scale than your competitors, then that means you can produce at a lower cost and if you can produce at a lower cost, you can sell those items at a lower price and still make an interesting return on your investment. This feeds a positive feedback loop in which the company that has the largest economy of scale can continue to extend that cost leadership. In that world, it makes sense that those companies that are very product-centric care about understanding the product and producing the product more efficiently. But Porter says there's an alternative way to compete: that is through differentiation. It's in that world where it becomes really important to understand your customers. Because in that world you need to produce a product with certain features that are more attractive to one set of customers. Then by definition, you need to understand that set of customers, what they want, and how much they're willing to pay for that.

Exactly, and I think that sounds like a second step. The first step is to understand who your customers are and where that 80/20 rule actually is for each customer. The second step is to then get into the needs and motivations of those valuable customers so that you can offer more value to them. Would you agree?

Colmenares: Absolutely. The whole customer centricity project begins with understanding the value of your customers, and that exercise of understanding the value of your customers is much more than just an accounting exercise or a prediction exercise. Once you understand who your most valuable customers are and who your least valuable customers are (who are often unprofitable) then you need to understand the differences in the needs and motivations of those two sets of customers. The insights are often shocking. The first one is the wide disparity, the wide heterogeneity, in the value of your customers. Companies are often surprised to find that 80 percent of their profits are generated by 10 or 20 percent of their customers and companies are often surprised to find that their least valuable customers are actually unprofitable. People in the beginning are often resistant because they can't believe it. It goes against the conventional wisdom that they've always been taught.

If I've only got 20 percent of my customers that are (and 20 percent might be generous for some companies) holding up the sales of my business, how can I create impact out of that small group to create a healthy company in the long term?

Colmenares: I run into this often when I speak to my counterparts at other companies, and this is relevant for marketing. Once you understand who your best customers are, who your most valuable customers are, their needs and motivations, and how those are different than those of the low-value customers, then you can start developing marketing campaigns to acquire more of the buyers that look like your existing best buyers. The company can put in place a set of actions to better retain the existing buyers that are the most valuable buyers. That might bring up the next logical question, which is, "What do we do with the remainder of the customers who don't fit the pattern of the very valuable buyers?" and the answer is by no means do you fire them. You just keep serving them as long as it doesn't cost you much to serve them. The insight here is spend your limited resources on the customers that are going to give you the highest ROI. Spend little to no resources on those customers that aren't giving you that great of a return.

So how does all of this apply to the customer retention game?

Colmenares: In my experience, people at companies will see tremendous opportunity in getting low-value customers to engage a little bit more and to essentially become more valuable. I feel this is a common mistake because the realization that companies need to arrive at is there's a reason why those low-value customers only engaged once or twice. And the reason most likely is because the value proposition does not resonate strongly with them. Often, it's a wasted effort to try to get these low-value customers to broadly migrate up.

That's slightly different than a customer-centric company who truly understands who their best customers are. Identify those diamonds in the rough, that small group of people within that group of 50 percent, 40 percent, or 30 percent of low-value customers identify those people that for reasons the company understands haven't migrated up. And if the company carries out some very targeted campaigns and very targeted actions towards migrating those diamonds in the rough to become high-value buyers, that's doable. But the general proposition of blanket targeting everybody who is a low-value customer and trying to migrate them up is a difficult proposition to actually execute on.

If people are going to churn, there's a reason why. Something's changed in their lives; they just aren't your customer anymore.
Colmenares: Exactly. No marketing is going to change that. The question is: What is the opportunity cost of that? Would the ROI of that investment be higher if I had used those resources to target a more valuable buyer for acquisition or to retain a high-value buyer? What is the opportunity cost of targeting these low-value buyers?

I love that phrase, "opportunity cost." It's something we rarely think about because we only look at what we spend. We don't look at the opportunity for what we could have spent in other places. That's a good way to think about it.
Colmenares: That often happens. There are two ways to solve the churn or retention problem. One is kind of the brute force, spend tons of money on that wide and large group of customers that aren't engaged and just try at all costs to get them to engage again. But a smarter way to do that is to solve the problem before acquisition. In other words, target the right buyers in the first place, which means that if you bring those right buyers, those customers are going to have much longer lifetimes with the company.

They're going to spend a lot more, and essentially your ROI is much higher. You're spending relatively less on acquiring those customers in order to get a much higher return. Companies need to stop focusing on what the cost of acquisition is and more on what the cost is relative to the value that that customer is providing to the company.

What if I've bought into this idea, I'm taking the next steps, and I understand the value of my customers and who my high- and low-value customers are. How do I get adoption within the company?
Colmenares: There are two things that are important to mention here. The first one is that it is absolutely critical to have buy-in from the company's leadership. You need to ensure that not only are the troops excited about this, but the leaders of the company are putting in place the goals and the policies so everybody's aligned and rowing in the same direction.

Are you saying leadership as in the C-suite levels or leadership as in somewhere else?
Colmenares: Yes. C-level all the way up because often what I find with people I speak to is that the product-centric conventionalism in the leadership of company is often very tied to that view of the world. You absolutely need buy-in from the leaders. The second thing is if one can't convince the leaders of the need to view the world this way, then what one can do is at least try to get buy-in for a few experiments to test it out, a few small-scale pilots that won't hurt the company if the pilots don't prove to be successful.

Is that the same path that you found was successful at eBay? Try some small experiments, gain the data, and then convince them?
Colmenares: Absolutely. It required small-scale pilots that wouldn't hurt the company if the experiments weren't successful and then with those first few experiments that were successful, we earned the right to do slightly larger experiments, and now we're running on much bigger actions.

Jaime's interview reflects the fundamental concepts of customer-centric thinking versus product-centric thinking. Customer-centric metrics focus on loyalty and lifetime value. When the metrics an organization is driving to are product-centric (e.g., number of widgets sold), it becomes difficult for customer-centric thinking to take root. I was pleasantly surprised to hear Jaime echo my own thoughts that a customer-centric transformation has to be led from the top.

In the next chapters, we will talk about ways to build up a customer-centric transformation. Note that the tactics begin deep in the organization at the analyst level with reporting (Listening Zone) and move upward to the director level with experimentation (Learning Zone) before ultimately arriving in the C-suite as innovations (Leading Zone). This provides a clear map to data value for senior management, who ultimately lead the customer-centric change.

• • •

CUSTOMER-CENTRIC TAKEAWAYS

→ Customer-centric thinking is predictive and quantitative. It is not the same as product-centric thinking. This difference is most notable in the way a company measures performance.

→ Customer equity not only reflects the health of a company, but also measures the goodness or quality of the base.

→ Customer equity, as measured by CLV, is the "North Star" of business metrics.

CHAPTER 2

The Path To Customer-Centric Transformation

LET'S BEGIN by differentiating customer-centric transformation from digital transformation. Digital transformation is heavily anchored to new technology upgrades (and the people and processes that support it). *Digital transformation* is important and often foundational, but the term undervalues the customer. A *customer-centric transformation* acknowledges the power of high-quality customers and seeks to build the long-term health of the business through the quality of the customer base ultimately measured as customer equity. High-quality companies have healthy customers.

The framework for customer-centric transformation (and also this book) is something I refer to as the *customer-centric maturity curve*, which you can see in Figure 2-1 (see next page). This is a handy way to diagnose the appropriate solutions for your company. (To that end, I provide a simple but powerful assessment tool in this chapter where you can apply it.)

As you can see, the customer-centric transformation is framed by the completeness of your customer view on the left or Y-axis and the speed with which you can take action on the right or X-axis.

FIGURE 2-1

Customer-Centric Maturity Curve

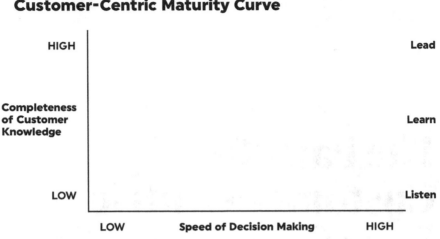

Looking at Figure 2-2, you can see the roadmap for customer-centric transformation.

The formulation of this path is the result of over 100 in-depth interviews with customer-centric leaders (some included in this book), industry knowledge, C-level conferences, and my personal experience. I have found repeatedly that companies who take on tasks ahead of their maturity typically fail until the foundational elements are filled in. Whether we like it or not, most companies take more than five years

FIGURE 2-2

Customer-Centric Maturity Curve

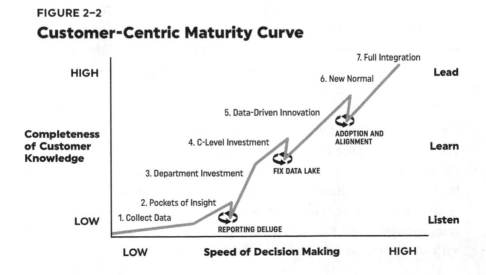

to mature in culture, skills, and leadership point-of-view. My goal is to provide you with the clearest path so your company can rise to competitive and financial advantage.

There are seven stages to the journey grouped into three zones. For the sake of clarity, I'll commonly refer to low or high maturity in each zone instead of the stage names. The earliest stage is the *Listening Zone*. This is where we learn to gather and shape customer data signals. The middle stage is the *Learning Zone*. This is where we begin to form and test hypotheses about why our customers (and non-customers) do what they do. Last, the *Leadership Zone* is where we begin to stand on the results of these tests to create algorithmic leadership and ways of working that lock in our competitive advantage. In this chapter, I'll cover the customer-centric transformation journey and the three zones a company passes through to get there. Let's explore each zone in more detail.

The Listening Zone

From the customer's perspective, a company in the Listening Zone is not listening well at all. While most companies have a call center or run surveys, what constitutes listening from the customer perspective is a comprehensive understanding across interaction points. At this stage, the experience is disjointed. For example, a local hospital I love has very high-quality doctors on staff. I gave birth to my second child here in the emergency room. But as pleasant as the staff were and as kindly as they cared for us, the birth was treated as a one-time event. The baby's future pediatric care, my own women's healthcare, and any prior experiences I had at the hospital were not connected. The burden was on me, the customer, to navigate and champion my care and that of my new family.

Contrast this to the more customer-centric hotel industry that is currently thinking about how to retain your loyalty by projecting your favorite pictures as wall art as you enter your hotel room in different cities! This requires the hotel to know who you are across properties as well as touchpoints to understand how you might feel, and to be willing to take a specific action. From a data perspective, the hotel must identify and classify you, know when you are due to arrive, when you've checked in, when you've used your mobile app to unlock the door to your room, and then display pictures with your express permission.

The hotel example shows what is possible. But, before you can build any kind of customer-centric strategy, you need to be able to hear and digitally "see" customers by collecting the signals they leave behind. Although these signals exist across many touchpoints, most are richly sprinkled throughout the marketing department, so that will be our start. And your analysts are usually the first to see them.

FIGURE 2-3
Listening Zone
Where companies refine their ability to listen to customer signals.

As pictured in Figure 2-3, the Listening Zone is about the initial collection and early usage of customer data. When marketing data starts to flow through an organization, nothing really seems to fit together. The paid search report doesn't fit together with the transactional report, which likely does not fit with the social media report or the website report. Ultimately, you end up with tons of reports and very confused stakeholders who plead, "Could you please just put this information together so that we understand what to do?" Compounding this problem is a lack of internal process which may make the data untrustworthy. I'll show you how to leap over this trap and create customer-centric reporting in Chapter 3.

The Learning Zone

From the customer's perspective, a company in the Learning Zone offers some inconsistent delights. These companies test and try new ideas, but it's not yet a wholly unified strategy. The more consistent this strategy becomes, the more customer-centric they are. Both Disney and Amazon have spent so many years learning from their customers, they have practically turned it into an art form. They are constantly experimenting to find and apply new innovations (e.g., Disney's MagicBand; Amazon's automated Go stores). They are highly customer-centric in both data and consistent "test and learn" strategy before execution. Contrast that with United Airlines which seems to have both inconsistent customer-focus and data. Just when one customer-centric PR disaster settles down, another one occurs (remember the "United Breaks Guitars" example you read about in the introduction?). The Learning Zone is about aligning data streams to test and release customer-centric programs.

FIGURE 2-4

Learning Zone

Where companies test and learn about customers based on captured signals.

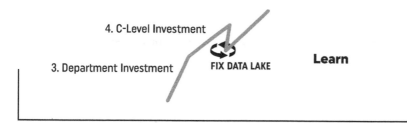

As you can see in Figure 2-4, the Learning Zone begins with departmental investment and alignment as the marketing reports interlock internally and then across teams. The challenge in this zone is aligning the company for both the input of more cross-departmental customer data as well as the coordinated output of customer-centric actions. Directors and VPs take on the bulk of the work, but this is where C-level oversight is needed in the form of a chief analytics officer, chief customer officer, or sometimes a CEO to emphasize cross-departmental support. Companies struggle to knit customer data together along with thorny issues of governance and access. The three-part union of customer-centric marketing signals, financial data, and technology comes together to initialize a virtuous cycle, sometimes referred to as the "customer-centric flywheel," which propels the company into the Leadership Zone. The *customer-centric flywheel* is a virtuous cycle of happy customers returning again and again. Although it may begin as a transactive event, the best companies turn it into an emotional bond.

The Leadership Zone

From the customer's perspective, a company in the Leadership Zone is a total delight. These companies have created a mutually beneficial relationship and often seem to be one step ahead in knowing customers' needs before they know them. For example, Uber's traffic analysis brings more drivers into the mix when surges occur. Domino's Pizza app sends well-timed, gamified promotions, then tracks your order from the oven to the driver to the (estimated) moment you begin eating. That's customer-centric algorithmic thinking.

FIGURE 2-5

Leadership Zone

Where companies innovate based on customer data and pull away from competition.

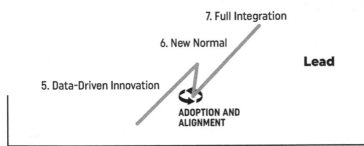

As you can see in Figure 2-5, the Leadership Zone begins with data-driven innovation, moves through the new normal, and finally transitions into full integration. It's the endpoint of customer-centric culture change assisted by algorithmic leadership for competitive advantage that has been percolating all along. At this point, customer-centric thinking has taken root and the senior management of the company regularly reviews data that pairs the health of the business with the health of the customer base.

The journey to customer-centricity does not happen overnight. It is important to keep moving forward to maintain market advantage. If you are not listening to, learning from, or leading your customers, you can bet your competition is. That includes the competitors you know as well as the fast movers that you haven't yet seen coming.

Assess Your Customer-Centric Maturity

Knowing where you are on the customer-centric maturity curve can help you build revenue and cultivate high-quality customers that result in customer equity. Remember: Customer equity creates real dollar value for companies. It's built from individual customer lifetime values. The way we listen to and respond to customers in our everyday actions helps create good experiences which, in turn, feed lifetime value. The collection of each customer's lifetime value added together is customer equity.

Let's talk a bit more about the three zones companies experience on a customer-centric transformation journey: listening, learning, and leadership. Each zone contains a few questions. Grab a notebook or open a spreadsheet document and count how many "yes" answers you get on the following eight questions. In the following chapters, I'll dig into each one in greater detail. For now, we will start with one question plus the most important piece of advice for that part of the transformation journey.

Listening Zone Assessment

1. *Do you trust your data?*

   By data, I mean all that digital deluge that's coming in. If you said "yes," move on. If you said "no," you are at the Low Listening Zone. What should you do? You should focus on tools. You need to validate and start tracking and collecting digital data from all channels like your email channel, customer service channel, website, or any channel you can access.

2. *Did you make at least one decision based on your digital data this month?*

   If you said "yes," move on to the next question. If you said "no," you are in the High Listening Zone. You should focus on hiring an analyst and beefing up your data collection tools, especially the voice of the customer. I often recommend analyzing the voice of the customer early because there's nothing that gets movement like a bunch of customers complaining about a bad process or needing help in a certain area. **The voice of the customer is powerful.**

3. *Do you have an overwhelming number of departmental reports that do not fit together?*
   If you said "no," and all of your reports fit together nicely, then move on to the next question. If you said "yes," that you get all of these reports and don't know what to do with them, then you are at risk in the Pit of Reporting Despair. You need analysis and expertise that focuses on humanizing the data. We often do this through use cases that approximate human behavior and task completion.

Learning Zone Assessment

1. *Do all of your marketing channels appear in one report using the grain of the customer or proxies of customers for both identified and unidentified people?*
   If you said "yes," move on to the next question. If you said "no," you are in the Low Learning Zone. At this stage, you really need process around governance to help align your teams and avoid sliding backward. Campaign governance that provides clarity on how customers found you is probably the first place to look. That's not the end of it but it's a good place to start.

2. *Can you see a complete view of your customers interacting across your business in sales, marketing, business intelligence or finance, and call center or support? Can you tell how much revenue they represent based on individually calculated—not averaged lifetime—value?*
   If you said "yes," move on to the next question. If you said "no," you are in the High Learning Zone. You are almost ready for a

chief analytics officer or chief data officer to help orchestrate data requests and publish meaningful insights. You also need technical support to land the data together as well as get better analysis and support for a cultural change from quantity to quality marketing. A recurring experimentation process helps to form a strong internal point of view about your customers. Connecting internal business knowledge to experimentation and analysis helps your customer data make sense. **In the end, you must be able to identify who is a good customer and who is a bad customer and the traits associated with each.**

3. *Is there a fast-connected data system that pulls each piece of customer data together from every corner of the organization?*
   If you said "yes," move on to the next question. If you said "no," then you are at risk in the Fix Data Lake stage. You need immediate next-generation technical tools sponsored by a senior executive such as a chief data officer or a chief analytics officer. These tools are not small. They are not lightweight to manage. They are big efforts that must get underway to make your data sing. There are some great new integrated systems that move faster than before, so in no way should you be talking about a five-year project, but you are talking about a very robust project. This technology forms the cornerstone of algorithmic leadership.

Leadership Zone Assessment

1. *Has each member of the executive team agreed to be measured by a set of specific metrics that interlock with company strategy and align to customer-centric tactics?*
   I want you to think about this specifically by the metrics. Every company has goals, but this is saying that there are specific measurable tactics that interlock with strategy. So, if you said "yes," move right along. If you said "no," you are in the Low Leadership Zone. It takes time to organize and gain commitment from other executives about what these numbers will be. Who's going to be held accountable? How are they measured? How do

they align the organization? There are very few companies in this stage, but they are the ones who confidently disclose specific customer metrics on their investor calls.

2. *Does everyone in every department understand and are they individually accountable for this same set of specific companywide metrics that are continuously measured and specifically laddered from tactic to customer equity evaluation or complimentary goal?* If you said "yes," then you are up there with the best of the best. I have yet to hear of any company who has operationalized customer equity across every department from HR to product to back-end operations. Now, if you said "no," you are not alone. This is the staying power behind long-term cultural change behind the customer-centric transformation in the High Leadership Zone. The primary need here is continuous socialization, use, and accountability. People know that this is the new normal and they are accountable for it.

You might have noticed that the questions got more complex and addressed more senior executives as they progressed. This is because like any good transformation, you must align at the top.

Why should you calculate your position on the journey to customer centricity? Because where you are determines what you need right now.

Transformational Tactics Defined

In the following chapters, which are focused on the zones you've been introduced to already, I am going to share a series of stories to illustrate how companies move through the customer-centric journey. See if one sounds like your company. Each story includes the fundamental framework of leadership, people, process, technology, and metrics. Let's define these framework elements before you dig into the zone chapters:

Leadership is important when it comes to getting organizations to drive by the data, which means teams feel comfortable making decisions based on the data. So, our first element is leadership as measured by organizational strategy, alignment, and innovation around the customer portfolio. It's the driver of the car with a firm, internally generated point of view.

People is often associated with skills and that's important, but what really matters are the actions that people can take and the leverage they have. So, we're going to talk about people's actions as measured by their behavior, which is the usage of tools and the output for customer-centric decisions. They are the wheels. Imagine what happens when they are not pointing the same direction!

Next, *Process* is measured by the ability to support and execute optimizations around the customer. It's the grease in the wheels that makes the car go faster or grinds it to a halt. It's not glamourous, but you won't get there without it.

Technology is measured by the flexible enablement of customer-centric business goals. These are the enhancements to the car, the catalytic converter, the ABS braking system, or the power steering. The failure of one system can make other jobs harder. Too many systems can also gum up the works.

Finally, *Metrics* synthesize our ability to listen, learn and lead for the mutual benefit of company and customer. Metrics help us see and celebrate success. This is the car's dashboard, but also the rear-view mirrors that tell you when you've left the competition behind.

So, with those definitions in mind, let's jump into the Listening Zone, and our first story, which is about the Kohler Co.

● ● ●

CUSTOMER-CENTRIC TAKEAWAYS

➔ Based on over 100 interviews, there is a specific pattern of customer-centric maturity most companies follow. They tend to get stuck in the same places and accelerate in the same ways.

→ While there are many micro stages along the journey, the macro trends can be divided into three zones: Listening, Learning, and Leadership.

→ Each zone begins with a story, outlines common traits, provides specific tactics, and then wraps up with another story illustrating the successful transition.

CHAPTER 3

Zone 1: Listening To Customer Data Trails

DOES THIS sound like your company?

Kohler Co. is located in Kohler, Wisconsin, right outside Sheboygan where the winters are cold, but the people are friendly and warm. Founded in 1873 by the Kohler family, this American manufacturing company is best known for plumbing products, but the company also manufactures furniture, cabinetry, tile, engines, and generators in addition to running Destination Kohler which manages luxury resort properties including The American Club Resort Hotel in the village of Kohler, Wisconsin.

With a 1967 advertising campaign, "The Bold Look of Kohler," Kohler established an early set of customers who love their products among builders, architects, and designers. To support these customers, the 36,000 square foot Kohler Design Center was built in 1985 to provide inspiration for the use of Kohler products. The search for inspiration still permeates most of Kohler's sites, which show creative and colorful uses of various products. In a 2015 issue of *Builder* magazine, which appeals largely to builders, designers, and architects, the brand was cited as the "most used" and "best quality."

This strategy was fine until a wave of empowered customers came online in 2006 with their mobile phones, social media-shared product reviews, and Amazon-driven expectations. Suddenly Kohler, whose products were traditionally and almost exclusively sold through third parties such as The Home Depot and Lowe's, had no way to directly interact with these customers. Like many manufacturers at the time, the lion's share of their revenues came from distributors. To sell directly to consumers would be to challenge relationships that held the bulk of their revenues. Kohler waited. Slowly 2006 became 2016. Kohler now faced uncontrolled pricing and resale of its products across the internet from approximately 200 sellers. In response, it finally launched an authorized etailer program and accepted only 17 online reseller partners. Alongside this program, Kohler finally began selling direct to consumers through Kohler.com.

If you were a customer trying to buy direct from Kohler before 2016 (when most companies had some ecommerce) you would have been very frustrated. The industry jargon used to describe products to designers and architects was similar but not the same as consumer language. Return policies and warranties were inconsistent across the internet. And even if Kohler had wanted to, they did not have robust systems set up to find a rare product, ship to someone's home, install products, or provide post-purchase support outside of their reseller network. Kohler had plenty of focus groups listening to builders, architects, and designers, but they could not take in or digest the avalanche of consumer data. In one attempt, the company created an entire war room of social media dashboards with real-time data streaming through. After the novelty wore off, few executives looked at the data and none understood how to take action on it.

Diamond (not their real name) began working at Kohler as a digital analyst around 2010. As a member of the centralized digital marketing team, they were tasked with providing "actionable insights" from website behavior for all parts of Kohler's business. But there was just one problem: Few of the executives trusted the digital data and even fewer felt comfortable to take action on it. Kohler marketing was under constant pressure to drive sales. Diamond diligently worked to integrate each tool with the data and monitor subsequent improvements. Deep-dive analyses and segmented visitor behavior were used to form logical experiments.

They measured results and outlined recommendations complete with screenshots, arrows, and competitive comparisons. But these intelligent findings languished with executives. Eventually, after Diamond felt they were asked to do their boss' work but was not subsequently promoted, they left to join a company that was more invested in using digital data. Diamond's departure was preceded by three of the six people on the digital marketing team.

Like many companies in the Listening Zone, the presence of powerful brand equity and strong distribution partners can suppress interest in customer data analytics. This is not wrong—it is simply a reflection of the historic business engines. But it does create an internal cultural challenge that is not fully resolved until you reach the Learning Zone, as we will see later.

In this chapter, you will learn the common traits of companies in the Listening Zone, how reporting becomes a tool for transformation, whether a customer data platform is right for you, and several ways to more powerfully shape digital data to sound more like customers. At the end, I'll review specific tactics related to technology, processes, leadership, people, and metrics.

Common Traits of Companies as They Enter the Listening Zone

As you can see in the Kohler example, Diamond's efforts did not bring the company out of the Listening Zone. Here are some traits you can see in companies as they begin their journey in the Listening Zone:

- There is a general mistrust of the data and confusion about what to do with it if anything.
- Technologies that allow executives to hear each customer's digital signal are light or missing.
- In rare cases where quality analysis breaks through, the culture makes taking action a risky career move.
- Leaders are not yet held accountable for taking action on data and as a result, the highest-paid person's opinion (a.k.a. "Hippo") will control strategic decision making.

- People who understand how to configure listening technologies are missing, so digital signals—especially about customers—is reported in silos.
- Supporting processes are spotty or non-existent.

If this sounds like your company, you are not alone. The process to becoming more customer-centric will be long but taking the right steps, particularly around reporting, will expedite your journey.

Did COVID Accelerate Kohler?

Companies who had digital ecommerce systems enabled clearly had a leg-up coming into 2020's COVID crisis. Fortunately, Kohler did launch ecommerce capabilities prior to COVID. Customer-centric features include automatic identification of your local store, encouraging customers to register to save design ideas and speed checkout, as well as helpful visualization tools and reviews. COVID forced many companies to reconsider a direct-to-consumer (DTC) approach and, perhaps for the first time, experience the power of direct consumer purchases. If COVID forced some companies to move forward, what holds them back?

Reporting As a Transformation Tool

In the Listening Zone, reporting is the primary method to understand customers. Reports are usually descriptive ("what happened") but can also contain some limited predictive measures. Using reports well can enhance your customer-centric transformation. But first, let's lay out some common misconceptions that block or at least slow down the transformation at this stage:

1. *We're busy building reports!* Sometimes it takes a lot of budget and time to build an amazing report that nobody uses. Part of this is cultural, but part is just getting to know the data. A common mistake is to think of a report as an endpoint, rather than an agile process that supports cultural change and learning.

2. *We need a dashboard!* Although a dashboard and a report are often synonymous, I tend to think of a dashboard as a collection of multiple reports. The thinking behind a dashboard is that it should arm the stakeholder with all they need to take action. What it usually does, however, is repeat information available elsewhere, and sometimes that can be helpful. Before investing, consider the right tool for the outcome. A report (or a dashboard) is not an analysis, nor is it an alert. A common mistake is to assume the solution for everything involving data is a report.

3. *We need a measurement framework!* This request comes from the idea that if data is grouped in the right way, it will yield more relevant information and people will naturally understand what to do. This is partially true, and the danger is in the approach that seeks to classify every metric (like page views or click-through rates). Putting metrics into a framework is similar to taking all the products in a grocery store and grouping them by the food pyramid to understand what to eat. This sample measurement framework is the food pyramid which allows me to classify whether that tomato is a fruit or vegetable, and if it's a fruit, but it's tomato sauce should I mix it with other fruits like applesauce? Definitely not. Bringing this back to data, the definitions of "reach" or "acquisition" are equally murky and filled with exceptions. A common mistake is to build a measurement framework on metrics instead of what the metrics represent: People.

I nicknamed this set of challenges (which you read about earlier) the Pit of Reporting Despair after the movie *The Princess Bride* and it is a real budget-burner. A typical company will have dozens of reports coming from different channels (call center, advertising, website, surveys, events) which reflect different datasets that just don't fit together. Compounding this, different departments may employ different agencies or vendors for each channel who add more reports. More siloed technologies add even more reports. The marketing department usually experiences this first. None of the reports fit together, which creates more confusion and does not propel a customer-centric transformation. One of the best ways to accelerate through this stage is to shape data around people whether they are your customer yet or not.

Is a Customer Data Platform the Solution?

With over 100 Customer Data Platforms (CDPs) on the market such as Amperity, Exponea, and mParticle, there are now many seemingly easy options to unite your customer data. CDPs can be a tool to accelerate transformation, but I prefer to think of them as a steppingstone. Few of the late Learners and almost none of the Leaders use a CDP. Why is that? Yes, these companies have dedicated the budget, in-house teams, internal technologies, skills, and processes to ultimately change their culture to be "customer first." But what is even more important, these companies have a specific point of view on their customers which is not easily reflected in any "pre-packaged" system.

Companies that did select a CDP are now hopping from one CDP to another hoping that the next one will better suit their needs instead of fixing the root causes. In my opinion, CDPs applied at the wrong time will only delay the customer-centric transformation. The solution? If you are in the High Listening Zone and want to move into the Learning Zone, a CDP can be a good tool to help you along, but recognize it is rarely a long-term solution because customer-centric transformation must ultimately be a deeply internalized point of view first.

Hearing Customers Through Use Case Reporting

Fundamentally, companies in the Listening Zone must be able to listen to the data streams left by their customers. Listening begins with collecting clean data from websites, surveys, marketing channels, and every customer touchpoint you can possibly find. For most companies, the marketing department has many rich listening points. You can also find good data within the product and social media teams. But once that data is collected, pushing it together will not naturally yield insights. To drive a customer-centric transformation, data needs to reflect who is coming and what are they trying to do. In short, data must be humanized.

When a company has low customer-centric maturity, humanizing the data goes a long way to creating cultural change. Terminology from each silo permeates reports (page views, visits, likes, clicks) making it difficult to unite the data on the basis of reports alone. Instead of coaching stakeholders on industry jargon, we can talk about people who are trying to achieve a specific goal. Reports and analyses generated with this language spark a feeling of helpfulness and being "of service" to the customer, which is one of the core concepts of customer-centric thinking. This is why it's vital to focus on use case reporting.

What is *use case reporting*? Here's a quick overview. Every action taken on any digital asset your company controls flows through at the most granular level as a "hit" or basically one line in a log file. Whether a person is identified or not, they get a random ID. Attached to this ID are hundreds of dimensions including device data, IP address, location mapping, inbound campaign source, and much more. Most of this is cookie-based tracking, but the need to collect some anonymous identification to successfully serve customers will not go away, even if the identification is temporary or synthetic. Offline data such as kiosks or event scans flows into the same structure when joined to digital. That's use case reporting.

We can cluster data into common activities people are trying to complete. We may not know whether that person is a customer or not, but it does not matter at this early stage. The flow of actions clustered together creates a meaningful framework that describes people and what they are trying to do, which leads us to explore how we can help. By speaking in the language of people who are confused, people who are job seekers, people who beeline to a specific product, and people who are brand new to us, we create the paradigm for customer-centric action. Let's look at some examples.

eCommerce Use Case Example

Figure 3-1 shows an ecommerce site example where the audience is assumed to be made solely of customers and prospective customers. The visit traffic is split into mutually exclusive groups based on common behaviors.

FIGURE 3-1

eCommerce Use Case

Snow Focused	I'm viewing snowboarding products.	**11%**
Surf Focused	I'm viewing boardshorts, bikinis, or other swim products.	**20%**
Product Browsers	I'm browsing product pages without a clear intent.	**40%**
Sale Shoppers	I'm browsing products and saw at least one product on sale.	**17%**
Brand Learners	I'm viewing about, blog, or other brand pages and not product detail pages.	**4%**
Home Page Only	I see the home page and leave immediately.	**6%**

Other: 2%

For example, one group always goes to the sale content, so they are classified as "Sale Shoppers," but another group skips that and beelines to snowboarding products (but not surfing), so they are "Snow Focused." Still another group skims across the top pages of the site looking at multiple product categories but not viewing products or buying so they are "Product Browsers."

Gary Angel's book, *Measuring the Digital World: Using Digital Analytics to Drive Better Digital Experiences* (FT Press, 2015) goes into great detail about use cases. I've simplified the process here. The first step is to define each group and ensure there is enough meaningful volume. I prefer more than two but less than ten use cases where the traffic volume in any one case is less than 50 percent. This is, of course, a general rule of thumb and there are exceptions. Use case classification can be based on site visit or visitor, but using visit is easier and may be more productive if you assume one person (a visitor) can have different reasons to appear on the website (visits).

The next step is to examine the behavioral trends of each use case for friction such as recurring churn between pages (shipping details and product page, or continuous searching). Once behaviors are identified, baseline the typical behavior (11 percent of all customers do this and 60 percent of them are new), set a goal for improvement (we want to reduce confusion by 10 percent) and work toward it. If successful, not only will you relieve customer frustration, but you could also see a lift in sales as customers find what they need more easily.

Figure 3-2 shows us a different example used to inform a redesign when there was no cart, just a "Where to Buy" button. In this example, you can see the use cases have been rolled up into "macro" audiences above the visit level. This can be helpful to change the conversation to "purchase-focused customers versus product-seeking customers" instead of using the more granular use cases of "collection browsers" or "inspiration seekers." Again, this is anonymous behavior illustrating an intent. We do not truly know if this is a customer until we identify them, which we'll discuss in the Learning Zone.

Use case segmentation helps increase customer signal by scrubbing the noise from digital data streams so you can listen more carefully to the customers who are reaching out. When data is framed by customer behavior, even when they are anonymous, it can prompt better internal

FIGURE 3-2

Non-eCommerce Use Case Example

Product-Seeking Customers	**Inspiration Seekers**	I view inspiration rooms or collections and do not view a product detail page.
	Collection Browsers	I view a category, collection, or search results page and do not view a product detail page.
	Product Browsers	I view a product detail page but do not view where to buy.
Purchase-Focused Customers	**Serious Product Browsers**	I view a product detail page and view where to buy.
	Where To Buy Focused	I visit where to buy and do not view a product detail page.
Non-Customers	**Brand Learners**	I view basics, newsletter, eco-thinking, or designer bio pages and do not view a product detail page.
	Home Page Only	I view the home page and immediately leave.

conversations about how to help them. It is even possible to break a few data silos down—especially within the marketing department—by adding more data to the use cases. For example, cross-department data sharing could knit together "click-to-call" data from the call center, ad spending details from the marketing department, or return data from a business intelligence group. Use cases create a valuable framework that yields a bigger picture of customer behavior before and after conversion.

Use case reporting creates a customer-centric eye for data and socializes stakeholders to frame data around the customer. "Are product seekers using this feature?" is a much more powerful question in the Listening Zone than, "Shouldn't we have more page views on this product?" Finally, use case segmentation provides signals about quality customer engagement. For example, when evaluating campaign performance, the percentage of serious product-intent shoppers versus the product-confused is a useful metric. In the Learning Zone, this adds additional context to advanced customer analytics strategies.

Insights Empowered Through Campaign Tagging

Campaign tagging is a powerful way to push more insight through the customer data stream. Most people ask, "Can't we just use the refer?" which captures the URL from which a visitor originated. No, because it cannot carry the context you'll want for future customer analysis. To empower customer analysis, you should add internal knowledge to your data. One of the first places to add it is in the campaign tag, like which customer segment you are targeting or why a customer does not appear unless you add it. Although campaign tagging is commonly used in marketing, it can be used offline (QR codes, shortened links which drive to landing pages), internally (internets or kiosks) or anywhere you put a hyperlink (public investor presentations). There are many paths up the mountain, but marketing is a good place to start because it has clear customer trails.

A campaign tagging (also called a campaign code) is public information, as you can see in Figure 3-3:

FIGURE 3–3
Campaign Tagging Example

In Figure 3-3, above, everything after the first "?" or query string parameter is a campaign tracking code. This appears after clicking on a link. In this case, I clicked on a paid search ad for Purple mattresses. The structure used by Google Analytics contains "UTM" and typically includes parameters such as the originating channel or refer (utm_source), the category within that channel such as organic or paid search (utm_medium), and the campaign name (utm_campaign). Anything that supports a hyperlink can contain a campaign code.

What kind of information could be carried by this code?

- What channel issued the offer (call center, sales team, or social media influencer)
- Which person in that channel issued the offer (Joe in sales, Ahmed in the call center, Jasmine in social media)
- Whether this offer was meant for new customers or loyal customers
- Whether you were targeting a specific interest or location
- Whether this offer was the result of an attempt to repair or rescue the customer
- Whether this offer was part of a larger multi-channel initiative or theme

Again, none of that information comes into the data stream. It's what I call "tribal" information, meaning everyone in the department knows about it, but an analyst who may be looking at the data collectively or years later will have no idea what happened *unless* there is a signal in the campaign codes. The campaign name is the easiest and most flexible to customize. Here's an example where the campaign name carries the purpose (e.g., acquisition, awareness, retention), geographic targeting (e.g., Southern California, New York, West Coast), and product promotion (e.g., black tees, white tees, striped socks):

FIGURE 3-4

Campaign Tagging

Clean campaign codes generate easy to understand campaign data.

acquisition — southern california — black tees

acquisition — southern california — white tees

acquisition — new york — white tees

retention — west coast — sock owners

acquisition — west coast — striped socks

awareness — new york — ambassador profile

awareness — southwest — ambassador profile

acquisition — southwest — white tees

acquisition — new york — black tees

Notice in Figure 3-4, that ambassador profile has been substituted for product in a few cases. This illustrates the vast flexibility of campaign naming. These values are typically human created but processed by machines later, so consistency is important. A consistent point of view on what to track in your campaign codes and when to change it will help to properly group and report performance.

LEARN MORE

Changes in Cookie Tracking

Most digital tracking is executed with cookies, those small files that reside on your browser when you accept or decline the "use of cookies" policy. Cookies issued by third parties are commonly used by advertisers such as Google. "Third party" simply means the tracking cookie is owned by another company. It does not match the site you are on, for example, when Google AdWords displays ads as you visit a news website. First-party cookies mean the tracking cookie is owned by the site you are on. First-party cookies are not going away. These are functional and marketing performance cookies, again, owned by the company whose site you are visiting. You can still accept or decline these cookies—or even purge them from your browser later—but overall, these cookies are used to improve your experience. All references to tracking in the Listening Zone and beyond relate to permissioned data stored as first-party cookies.

Tactics That Transform Listeners to Learners

As we entered the Listening Zone, the stakeholder was deep in the organization, perhaps a senior manager asking: *Do you trust the data?* Have you taken action on it? The Listening Zone begins with technology and progresses to people's actions. There can be pressure for more results or "actionable insights" than the data can yield, unless correctly configured. The company begins to crave an impact from early technical investments, but this is held up by the misalignment of goals and metrics from a higher up in the organization. Instead, small sometimes sporadic wins occur based on the performance of a particular campaign activity or the optimization of a particular channel or part of the site. The conversation moves from, "We are going to optimize our paid search based on clickthrough" to "We are going to optimize our paid search terms to reduce product confused visitors." Ultimately, reporting is the tool that drives customer-centric change and allows stakeholders time to develop a trusted, actionable customer-centric perspective.

In the Listening Zone, leadership is not sure what is possible. Either a critical event like COVID comes along, a competitor begins to dramatically gain market share, or someone has a vision that sparks the desire to transform the organization. Foundational technology in this stage does not have an immediate or high return on investment and, therefore, it is not easy to prioritize. There is much work to do (and a bevy of tools and vendors trying to do it for you) that can make it hard to get going. To move forward, you will need to ask the following critical questions.

What Technology Should Support the Listening Zone?

Listening cannot begin without the right technology. Kohler adopted and configured listening technology through Adobe Analytics, then added both use case reporting and campaign codes that set the organization up for long-term success. The goal is to hear the customer through the capture of rich, robust data, and to monitor the quality of that data. Monitors enable trust, which allow teams to defend their early data-driven decisions.

Technology tools and vendors quickly increase to support the desire to understand and measure mostly marketing success. That may be a new tool that helps you orchestrate social media better. Or maybe you start using an SMS system to reach customers. That's all part of technology. As the volume of data increases, it inevitably connects to the core reporting system that is attached to the website in early days, or even a data warehouse. So, when you think about Google Analytics or Adobe Analytics, do not think about website tracking. Think of it as an early-data landing zone to help knit together anything digital which could include not only a website but a kiosk or an internet-enabled thermostat or badge scans at an event. So, when we talk about core reporting systems or digital analytics, we're really talking about the universe of everything that is connecting that into one central system. Moving forward, you can gradually marry this data to customer ID.

I also recommend voice-of-customer systems to start capturing more detail about what customers want. Some of this may come from the call center, from onsite surveys, or even external research. Just make sure there is an individual customer identifier present. Aggregated customer survey responses are not especially useful because we lose the ability to prioritize actions and directly measure revenue impact.

How Should Teams Take Action in the Listening Zone to Gain Traction?

Companies within the Listening Zone generate a lot of one-off reports. Common questions analysts receive are:

- How many visitors did we get to the website?
- How many visitors came through paid search?
- How many page views did a product receive?

These are good questions, but it can be exceedingly difficult for stakeholders to take action because more volume does not always mean more quality. Flip the script by changing to customer-centric use case reporting. Add extra power to your customer-centric insights through campaign codes.

How Should Executives Support the Listening Zone?

To gain continued momentum in the Listening Zone, a senior leader with vision needs to say, "Yes, we need to get in the game and here is where it is going to take us to long-term success." Top concerns may include managing the budget and spending priorities. When immediate ROI is thin because analysts are just scratching the surface of customer insights, the critical blocker to overcome is budget to maintain your progress. A strategic roadmap will help align your early vision and reduce the feeling that this is a "leap of faith."

What Processes Support the Listening Zone?

Processes may not be well-defined but if they are, it is mostly tactical: How do you set up paid search? Or how do you set up a campaign? Little is geared to the measurement or the optimization of the customer-centric data. Remember that "process" means you may be starting to set some customer-centric baselines and targets. You may be starting to understand what "good" looks like and that analysis is driven by the campaign governance and the tagging governance. A process is about bulletproofing trusted data. Reporting framed around people (about who's coming and what are they trying to do) tends to gain attention from a broader internal audience who want to help the customer, and that is critical for getting out of the Pit of Reporting Despair. This information, though still imperfect, drives a clearer line of sight to missing pockets of customer data, and that in turn drives the next stage of development.

What Metrics Support the Listening Zone?

In the Listening Zone, we monitor data quality and load speed to prevent companies from sliding back down the curve. These are defensive measures that protect your progress. In addition to the standard analytics reports you might receive, I recommend measuring custom ratios and defining use case segmentation to help expedite your progress. These are offensive measures that accelerate the customer-centric transformation. See Figure 3-5.

FIGURE 3–5
What to Measure in Listening Zone

Measures That Protect	Measures That Accelerate
Monitor Data Quality	**Custom Ratios**
• Site tracking [tool: verified data]	• Look-to-book or buy
• App tracking	• Net Promoter Score
• PII compliance	**Use Case Segmentation**
• Campaigns [tool: Claravine]	• Product engagers
Load Speed [tool: Pingdom]	• Product directed
	• Product confused
	• Brand focused
	• Land and leaves

How do you know when you have filled in the important gaps and completed the Listening Zone? Ask yourself these questions:

- Are stakeholders asking for specific data to support decisions which will be made?
  - Could you tell me how many people viewed my product page? (This is an example of a "Not actionable" question.)
  - Where did people come from who showed product confusion? (This is an example of an "Actionable" question.)
- Are more business owners demanding they need the data to make actionable business decisions, but it is taking too long to get it? Count the number of requests and time to fulfill times the fully loaded salary of a typical employee (2,080 working hours/$75K is $36/hour) and make the case to increase your budget.

If you answered "yes," then it is an excellent time to enter the next zone of customer-centric maturity: Learning. We'll cover that in the next chapter. But first, let's meet another leader who speaks to the world of customer-centricity: Peggy Winton.

How AIIM International Became Customer-Centric with Peggy Winton, President and CEO of AIIM International

Digital transformation (which you first read about in Chapter 2) begins with enhancing the customer experience. **Peggy Winton** knows this from personal experience at AIIM International, where she is currently President and CEO. She defines digital transformation in information terms and offers four key components of instituting organizational change around Customer Lifetime Value. Winton believes that this transformation gains a powerful start in the marketing department. It's all about relationship building and the intelligence of the customers that provides the true value. As I spoke with Peggy about her experiences with digital transformation, I wondered if customer-centric techniques would be equally valuable to a non-profit. Here is our conversation.

Peggy, we met at a digital transformation conference where we were both speakers, and I have to say it was really delightful to hear your clear commentary on not just marketing transformation, but digital transformation. Can you tell us a little bit more about your background and how you became CMO and then we can dig into that topic?
Winton: Absolutely. Thank you. And I feel the exact same way about your remarks on the lifetime value of the customer. I believe that digital transformation begins with this obligation we now have and this challenge to truly enhance our customer experience, so we have to focus on the value that we provide to our customers and the value they can provide to us and the members of our value chain and our supply chain. I came to my current organization 15 years ago. I came to AIIM right at the time when we were dramatically changing our business model from a single, annual, typical exhibition and conference. We sold that to an outside firm and essentially had to rebuild our portfolio. And I was brought in to do that. I remember early on saying, "Why don't we saddle with some of these old business models? Why are we acting like a charity? A nonprofit is not the same

as a charity, so why are we doing all these sorts of nicely-nicely things without driving value all the way around?" I remember thinking this could be the best thing that happens to this organization, or the worst thing, my bringing up a for-profit mentality.

And I think that's particularly interesting how you move from CMO to CEO, but you had that for-profit mentality. So really you came in to kick off a digital transformation before the term "digital transformation" was really used. Is that right?

Winton: You're absolutely right. The other aspect I think about digital transformation is doing things differently and doing different things. I probably had a huge advantage in coming in from the outside without a whole lot of predispositions and a lot of biases where the typical association of not-for-profit models come into play. I could look at things with a more critical eye, and I focused immediately on how we grow this community of ours and how we extract maximum value from that community. I should probably say that as an association, we serve both the users and the suppliers of information management technology.

So we serve two masters, and therein lies the challenge, but also the opportunity to say we had a lot of really good content. We were building this year-round portfolio of programs and activities that were based on curating that content and then surfacing that content. It didn't take long for me to realize that the old association model begins and ends with dues-paying members because that was a subset of the thousands of people we were touching with this content. And we set about really expanding that reach and trying to determine the value that we could place on people that, for whatever reason, didn't become a lifer or dues-paying member, but yet represented amazing value. Particularly for those suppliers in our space who wanted access to qualified customers.

When you went about the process of thinking about how to increase value for the organization or the value that the organization offers, how did you approach that question? How did you come to quantify the value?

Winton: It was kind of skunk works at the beginning. We didn't have a tool that could do that for us, but we tried to just begin with the history that we have. That's usually the best that any of us have to go on, so we, of course, had a transactional database. We started looking at what were those products of ours that we offered and who was buying. We could certainly put a value on that. We realized that it was not necessarily those dues-paying folks who had been in the industry for a long, long, long time, felt a sense of obligation, paid their dues, and then just probably didn't do that much to engage or to continue to deepen their relationship with us as a customer. We also looked at the value of those people consuming all of the free things that we do.

We do a webinar a week. We put out a lot of things like infographics and ebooks. The folks that we're engaging with those and permitting us to own their name basically provided immense value for the vendors in our space through wanted access to new buyers. So we tried to put a value on that about the monetization of that extended community of non-dues payers, and that's where the real light bulb went off for us.

Did you use that as a compass to drive your decisions or was it more of just a factor that fits into the overall thought process?
Winton: I think it changed everything for us. We started investing in marketing automation tools so that we could really leverage what we found out and make it go to work for us and allow us to scale. We're a tiny organization with about $5.7 million in revenues and about 23 people, so exceedingly small. We needed the tools to help us with that. It did become the very basis of our go-to market strategy, and we were able to tell that story to those suppliers in our space to get them excited about our community and this new crop of qualified buyers that they had at their disposal. Everything flowed from there and the very reputation of marketing within our organization changed. I always say people marketing is not about pretty pictures and there's no magic that happens in that regard. It really is all about the intelligence of our customers that provides the value for us.

That's a great place to start. Let's talk a little bit more about marketing, and maybe there are some examples you can share about how you went about the change with marketing or what areas you found were ripe for automation. How did you actually make it stick?

Winton: Well, thank you for asking that because that's probably one of the most exciting stories. It's an exciting story about the fact that the marketing automation tool in which we invested, that decision was completely driven by the business. In this case, marketing our albeit small bench had nothing to do with it, but it's probably the most successful project we've ever had because we knew what was required. We knew what was needed. We gathered a blended team to set those business requirements, and we chose a tool that really represents the way I think small-to-medium-size organizations should be purchasing: low code or no code, very small cost of ownership and easy to get started with right away. But that tool is considered a marketing automation tool and it very much is built on the philosophy of what's called "inbound marketing."

We were sending thousands and thousands of outbound emails, and that's just not good. If your very value is this community of customers that have endeared them to you, you certainly don't want to jeopardize that relationship by bombarding them with emails. So that was a very reasonable and easily understood goal that we had to try to reduce the number of emails.

We call that spray and pray. Spray them out and pray for results.
Winton: That's right, hope for the best. And so, the idea of inbound marketing is to let your content go to work for you in perpetuity by leveraging all the other outlets that we now have at our disposal to gather unknown people to us. And with that, I'm talking about social media and providing educational content so that people can find you, so when they find a piece of content that we have created, we always have a call to action that sends them to a landing page where we can capture just the details and the permissions that we need at that point and commensurate with the type of content that we are putting out there. Then we use the tool to do what's called "progressive

profiling," and we've deepened that engagement with nurturing campaigns that can be completely automated. Our customer downloads this little checklist that's just a one-pager, and then we always offer a secondary call to action to take it to the next step. We base everything now on activity and behavior, not profile. We let you determine the next step, and that makes for the very best customer.

Many people miss that subtlety of your trading value progressively over time, the progressive concept profiling. I'm asking you for a little bit of information because you're giving me just a little bit of information back and as the relationship deepens, I give you more information and you keep encouraging me to have a stronger relationship. It's a lot like classic relationship building, and that's a beautiful way to run marketing. It's what it should be, right?

Winton: Marketers can no longer just take the easy way out and do the least amount of effort. They may get away with it for a little while, but everyone's more and more sophisticated, including the very customers that we're trying to attract.

Are you free to name the marketing automation tool that you decided to go with?

Winton: I am, and there are many tools out there, but we have been absolutely delighted with a tool called HubSpot.

One of the challenges I think a lot of people have when they're running marketing is when they put all that content in place, and they get some progressive profiling. Did you have to feed in some sort of quantitative piece like LTV or value in order to decide the order of operations with which you presented information because you're trying to balance the health of the organization?

Winton: Oh, absolutely. And one of the things that I did when I became CEO was to get every single member of my staff comfortable with the profit and loss statement (P&L). That sounds so simple, and it might sound crazy to some, but why not? Why have any lack of transparency when it comes to how we make money and what programs are good business from a net margin perspective? And I think that's another fault of a lot of organizations. They get just completely attracted by the top-line revenues, but they don't realize all of the cost, including staff costs that go into that. We had to put that filter on everything we did, and I won't say for a minute that the tools that we use give us an instant view at the value of any one customer.

But there are a lot of different ways that we can manipulate the cumulative information to get a good picture there, and we do. For us, the key is automation again, because we're just so small. You're not going to get it perfect every time. You start with the personas that you can determine again from that historical basis, you go from there, and you determine what level they are in terms of their readiness to quote-unquote buy and just what their particular interests are. You do the best you can, and you keep looking and you keep tweaking and you keep doing it, but you can't get too granular, or you'll just drive yourself crazy.

Are there any other examples you want to share with us about the transformation of the organization, whether it's marketing or otherwise?
Winton: Someone said to me that digital transformation is rethinking the business that you're in. When new folks come on board with us (and I'm talking about staff) I always ask them, "What business do you think we're in?" And people will say, "Oh, well, you're, you're the community for information professionals." Yes, but that's not really what I have in mind. What else? And they'll say, "Oh, well, we're running an association. We are in the association management business." Yeah, but not really. What we realize is that we are in the marketing business and all of us are sales and marketing people, and that sounds mercenary. We are still a nonprofit. We hope that we're still fulfilling a mission and serving the needs, but we are first and foremost a marketing organization. And when you think about it that way, you start thinking, "Hmm. What are other offerings that we have?"

Maybe things we didn't even intend. And here's one example. We were collaborating with some of the suppliers in our space to be good thought leaders and help us put on a nice educational event and provide them with those permissions leads for their own needs. We realized why weren't we offering something even deeper as a consultant, knowing what we know about our own marketing automation tools and practices. So we started a whole other offering for those vendors in our space that wanted their own multitouch, multi-context, deep customer intelligence story that they could tell. We started a subscription annuity business. It's still within our industry, but it could be completely independent for vendors who are providing all kinds of other types of tools.

And that's been an addition to our portfolio of programs, and some would say that's sort of outside the association business. It's not because we're still serving those same suppliers, but it's an add-on using what we know and what we've learned from our own technology choices.

Well, not everyone may like that as an add-on, but most likely it's attracting a benefit to perhaps your most loyal or your premium subscribers: people who really want to go deep with your organization. So in a way it rewards both of you because it's an annuity. I love that you've used that word because many people who run businesses don't think in those terms and it's a fantastic recurring revenue stream. It's also allowing them to feel a stronger sense of special handling or kid-glove treatment. That is what we try to provide to the high-value customers.
Winton: You're so right, and we realize we're doing such a better service to both. You're quite right. Just like we knew that we couldn't just fire off a bunch of unrelated emails. Our suppliers certainly cannot and should not be doing that and this way we respect the end-user customer to say, "You get to choose how deep you want to take this, and we're going to respect you in that process."

Let's say that I'm excited about this idea of marketing transformation, and I want to do maybe not just marketing, but digital transformation overall. What kind of actions can I take?
Winton: We spent probably the better part of last year gathering

some of the best and the brightest in our community together to see if we could define digital transformation and then build a set of tools around that because it is one of those terms that everybody's probably tired of hearing. It means a lot of things to different people, or it means nothing to some people because it's almost viewed as a throwaway. We looked at our world, and we defined digital transformation in information terms because information is the currency that we deal in. The first one is this whole customer experience enhancement anticipating before they even tell you what they need, and we think that all things actually flow from there because the second one is innovating.

And when you think about the true disruptors in our space, it begins with figuring out where there is friction in the act of doing something that customers need every day. Uber knew that there was friction to the art or the act of hailing a taxi. They did, and it was in the name of customers to please them, to make their lives easier, to make it more convenient that that innovation was born. So, number two is innovation. Number three is we have got to digitalize all of our core processes because that again will stop good customer service in its tracks if there is a manual process that causes somebody to have to stop, get off their smart device and do something (heaven forbid paper-based or manual). And then the fourth thing is that, like it or not, we have to do all of those three things above while minimizing our risk.

And again, with the customer in mind, we now are under greater pressure to protect the customer data that we hold and to give them full control over how we use it. So that's what we did to define the digital transformation, and I think it applies to almost any business of any size and in any industry.

To summarize, we talked about how automation is the first place that your organization leads. You began with historic personas, got an understanding of the audience, and then moved into automation once you knew what you wanted. Then, we looked at how you created impact. That's the financial transparency. You give every single member of your staff access to the P&L and get them comfortable so that they are thinking long-term about the business that they're in, especially how to provide value with respect to the bottom line and respect to the customers. I think that's a really interesting balance. You're constantly pushing the customer relationship and value of the relationship, but at the same time, you're not walking away from the financials. Like we said earlier, it's not a charity. You're in business to provide value, and that value should appear on the bottom line.

Winton: That's right. I had to sort of right this ship when I joined because I think the focus was too much on that top-line revenue without looking at what was good business and what isn't. Much of what I did in creating this whole year-round portfolio was to think in bits, not bytes, so that we could administer and dispense them with the highest possible margin. Why wouldn't I want every member of my team to understand where those revenues and costs derive and how to be more creative about increasing and decreasing the other? Not surprisingly, the very best ideas and much more creative than my own have come from my team that with that information and the power of that has really allowed them to come up with some just some great new programming.

What I'm also hearing there is in addition to not just looking at the top line, you're also taking a longer-term view, not by looking at the bottom line alone, but also taking those ideas from the team and looking long-term at how the organization operates. Am I correct in that assumption?

Winton: That's absolutely right. I mean, somebody said for the not-for-profit world or the association world, we're not really in the business to make money. I challenged that because if we are without money in the bank, there's not much you can do. I always say profit is good even in a not-for-profit, so you've got to have a good financial structure that will allow you to then invest in things that maybe are a little bit little bit edgier, or maybe need a little bit of testing. I mean that's where the true differentiation comes. If you don't have any of that, it's pretty hard.

AIIM's digital transformation began when Peggy realized the high value of "customers" who were not dues-paying members. She surprised me when she showed how her non-profit clearly operated at the intersection of finance and marketing. Further, by listening to these customers' interactions and letting them lead the next request, AIIM was able to identify a steady stream of valuable content and services beyond the traditional membership dues model. AIIM's desire to "be of service" by deeply engaging their broader customer base instead of "pushing dues-paying memberships" is what initiated their customer-centric transformation.

• • •

CUSTOMER-CENTRIC TAKEAWAYS

- **Listeners first must trust the data before they are willing to take even low-risk actions.**
- **Surfacing "what happened" in a dashboard is only the starting point. Dashboards are informational tools that should be constantly modified to support cultural change.**
- **Shaping data to sound more like people who need help increases internal understanding and decreases jargon and distancing language.**
- **Actions taken to tune data in this zone continue to pay off when financial impact is added, especially as the company matures its customer intelligence.**

CHAPTER 4

Zone 2: Learning From Customer Data

DOES THIS sound like your company?

Nike was originally founded in 1964 by University of Oregon track-and-field coach, Bill Bowerman and his former student, Phil Knight. They opened their first retail outlet as Blue Ribbon Sports in 1966 and launched the Nike brand shoe in 1972. By 1980, the shoe name had become the company name and the brand went public as Nike, Inc.

Over the decades that followed, Nike, with the help of Portland agency Wieden+Kennedy who created the famous "Just Do It" campaign, mastered brand marketing. Before "influencers" referred to everyday people on social media, Nike recognized the power of athlete endorsements and lined them up across the key sports where the Nike products were sold. From their origin in running shoes, Nike expanded into basketball, soccer, tennis, golf, and then into extreme sports such as snowboarding and mountain biking.

Before the internet boom in the late 1990s, one successful way to build a business was to create a powerful brand, line up distribution on store shelves so people could buy the products of your brand, then add on with more products. This is known as *product-centric marketing*, and it is distinct from customer-centric marketing in the ways we discussed in **Chapter 1: Getting To Know Customer Centricity.**

In the early 2000s, as internet ecommerce was growing, Nike's new agency R/GA built a sexy website in Adobe's Flash language that included ecommerce. The only problem was, Flash was not trackable and because of this, Nike was basically blind to digital customer signals. Nike could not easily understand how visitors shopped, bought, or what drew them to the site. Like many major brands at the time, Nike wrestled with the question of, "How important is it to sell products direct-to-consumer from the website?" With more than 95 percent of sales coming from distribution channels such as Dick's Sporting Goods and Foot Locker, it was a delicate question for Nike.

But the question of how visitors were experiencing the website nagged at employees internally who could not answer executives' questions, and eventually a new trackable site was built and gradually launched in 2010.

Digital was hot and Nike soon spread into devices such as the Nike+ FuelBand and Kinect Training for Xbox. These systems collected usage data and customer data via the account login. The desire to understand more about customers increased, but because digital consumers (including website buyers) were so small in number compared to the massive physical distribution channels, the answers were thin. But buried behind the sexy brand-centric volume metrics of increasing social likes and page views, the one thing that did stand out was purchase velocity. Direct purchases on the Nike website were accelerating quickly. Nike's earlier question about disrupting their distribution channels gradually became less important. Consumers were showing up in droves at the Nike website. In response, Nike launched the "Know me to serve me" internal effort which officially kicked off its customer-centric focus.

Nike rapidly built on all the listening data it had collected and began actively experimenting with new ways to alleviate visitor frustration and pain. From errors found only on mobile devices to third-party payment systems that looped customers through a series of spaghetti pages to co-branded partner sites, terabytes of data were coming in fast. Nike's internal teams took hold. They tested and learned how to serve their digital customers. They stretched beyond data silos of website, call center, and social media, and gradually expanded their comprehensive view of the customer. They added an anonymous ID to all website visitors which resolved post-purchase to pre-purchase behavior. They meticulously outlined all the site features that were used and how much they contributed to conversion in order to forecast the impact of each test. Nike's tech team pulled in Cloudera, a fast and modern database built on the Hadoop storage and analysis clusters developed at Yahoo!. Customer data was married to Acxiom's broader U.S. consumer data set to understand Nike consumer profiles more clearly. In 2018, Nike acquired Zodiac, a customer-centric consumer data analytics firm to accelerate digital transformation using the predictive methods of CLV.

All that said, metrics and tech alone cannot cause a company to be customer centric. There is a deep cultural shift that must occur as well. Domino (not a real name) was a brilliant mid-level analyst at Nike as digital transformation initiatives picked up steam. Executives were seeking answers from the data almost as if it were a crystal ball forecasting weather, demand, consumer trends and more; questions were pouring in. Nike added analyst support as internal teams ran reports and analyses again and again in what seemed like a continuous series of fire drills. According to Domino, Nike executives had questions, but it appeared they did not always know what they would do to take action on the data. In some cases, the analyses fueled an internal competition where data produced for one team were not easily shared with another. In addition, Nike's planning process was so long and arduous that any analyses requiring nimble decision making and action was greatly delayed. One case Domino remembered was a trend-sensing model. The model correctly identified women's yoga pants as a multi-billion-dollar market opportunity. When Nike executives were presented with this information, the request was to wait nine months to see if the trend was accurate. Meanwhile, lululemon capitalized on Nike's inaction and became the biggest player in the segment. The yoga pants trend is now an everyday reality.

Nike's culture had to change, and it did unexpectedly. In 2018, accusations of workplace bullying and sexual harassment came to a head after a group of female Nike employees presented an internal survey on workplace behavior to CEO Mark Parker. Ultimately, eleven Nike executives were dismissed by Parker. But from Domino's perspective, the aggressive workplace culture ran deep. Their departure coincided with several other bright and powerful mid-level leaders who ran experiments, business intelligence, and digital analytics departments who despite the high quality of their work, could not get the data signal through the political noise. Most went on to lead admired data initiatives at well-known brands.

Customer-centric transformation is not only about the right tools, metrics, and technology. It reflects the internal culture of the company. In the Listening Zone, we saw how Kohler's powerful brand equity and strong distribution partners suppressed interest in customer data analytics. Nike was able to move beyond this when strong velocity was identified in the direct-to-consumer market, but still had to process internal cultural changes to make acting quickly on the data feel natural, which is not an easy feat.

In this chapter, you will learn the common traits of companies in the Learning Zone, how data lakes advance transformation, what customer lifetime value is, whether AI is right for you, and why experiments rapidly advance a company's ability to not only understand customers but to align the financial impact that solidifies cultural change. At the end, I'll review specific tactics related to technology, processes, leadership, people, and metrics.

Common Traits of Companies as they Enter the Learning Zone

When a company enters the Learning Zone, there is a marked desire for more data. The company sees value in the data and may have even taken low-risk actions on it. Here are some common traits that companies share at this stage:

- They stand on good processes and governance that secure foundational data for analysis.
- The pace of data-centric thinking increases which includes more sources and more questions.

- Test and learn will become a major driver of customer-centric understanding.
- Customers are more clearly identified.
- Some analyses are gaining the attention of executive leadership.

With the desire to use data more effectively comes the need to access it more efficiently. In the Learning Zone, data lakes support the transformation to customer-centric maturity.

Did COVID Accelerate Nike?

By 2020, as malls shut down and retail stores closed during the COVID crisis, Nike was finely tuned and ready to not only receive direct consumers en masse but to build a "deep and meaningful consumer connection," according to Nike's new CEO John Donahoe. Nike remains hyper-focused on long-term growth, which is a core customer-centric trait, but innovation at Nike continues to be product-defined. New products reach into the edges of the customer universe such as maternity wear and full-coverage modesty swimwear. The pandemic "stress tested" Nike's digital transformation strategy, according to Donahoe, moving their direct-to-consumer goals from 4 years to 2 years. Originally the company launched a Consumer Direct Acceleration (CDA) initiative whose goal was that 30 percent of sales be direct-to-consumer by 2023. After 2020, Nike was rapidly closing in on 50 percent direct-to-consumer sales. Through well-constructed data, Nike knows that heightened engagement equals not only higher CLV but that digital sales are accretive to the company's operating margin. In other words, not only is Nike selling more to consumers directly, but every sale is more profitable. This is leverage Nike will use to extend its competitive advantage. As a result, the company has shifted away from mass-market retailers and closer to innovative retailers that more accurately reflect the premium experience of the Nike brand such as the House of Innovation in New York and Shanghai, or Nike Rise, which is a neighborhood initiative. With new leadership, Nike is driving hard to illustrate its core values align with customer values.

Data Lakes As a Transformation Tool

In the previous section about Listeners, the fundamental need was to trust the data. Now, as companies advance to Learners, the fundamental need is for a fast, connected data system that pulls each piece of customer data together across the organization. That can be a tall order, especially in large companies.

In the Learning Zone, the database is the primary tool to understand customers. Some companies have advanced to a *data lake*, a massive landing zone for processed data, including customer data. Let me briefly explain the difference. In the 1990s when companies installed a database, it was a relational database. To stand up a relational database, the business intelligence or IT team went through a fairly large effort to map out relationships and keys so that specific information could be connected. For example, if you wanted to know which customer bought which product, you would have to have previously created a join between the customer and product tables. This process could be good for the CFO who might need the same reports again and again, but slow and messy for customer data analysis. No matter how well the relationships were mapped out, the data could change, creating a new need that had not been anticipated before. For example, if we add device type to the previous example of customer and product table, we would need a new table and a way to join it.

For executives hungry for answers, the long delay to produce this information meant it could easily be obsolete before they received it. Adding to the problem, follow-up questions may have been equally time delayed. However, some questions are predictable and repetitive (e.g., How many sales did the Mid-Atlantic region have this month?) so data warehouses are still important and useful.

As pressure mounted to answer executive questions quickly and the cost of data storage decreased, the data lake became a popular solution. Unlike the data warehouse, which structures data prior to use, the data lake captures unstructured data. This allows the query writer (often a data scientist) to assemble the pieces they need to answer executives' questions on demand. Using our previous example, adding device type to the customer and product table can be done by one person in minutes, not days or weeks. A successful data lake stores the wealth of the business in one place and includes a data dictionary to define the source of record and processes or calculations used to collect the data.

Customer data, including unidentified behavior of future customers, break data silos especially across business units, and encourage alignment around a common external cause. Every department with customer data also touches the customer but it is unlikely they've been asked to interlock it before. Learners put a process around governance to gather and create the keys to interlock the data. Keys are simply a piece of matching data. It could be a name, email address, or random series of numbers that is identical in two different datasets. That's all a key is. Often email is used as a key and an email address can be somewhat unique. Of course, the challenge is when the customer provides first name, last name, and email address, but then uses a different email address on the next purchase.

What some companies do is generate their own specific customer ID and try to match all the different bits of customer data into one ID. Once the keys interlock the data, the next need is to build high-speed data systems which can run queries, reports, and analysis at the customer grain.

Whether a company runs a database, data lake, or both, the problem that holds listeners back remains the same. Data has no natural intelligence, so putting it in a bigger pile is of limited use. For example, in Nike's case, early databases built in the U.S. and internationally did not have standard terminology for color. Whether a database or data lake was used, the bigger problem when trying to figure out how many red shoes were sold was trying to figure out what qualifies as "red."

Another common example where the same word has different internal meanings is the term "channel." What qualifies as a marketing channel could have multiple names and formats (e.g., eMail, e-mail, e mail, email) which is a governance problem but further, the sales team might also use the term "channel" in a completely different context (e.g., direct, wholesale, distributor). So, the first problem is consistent governance of the data. The second problem is that important context behind the data may not even be present in the raw data. For example, was this a limited-edition shoe or one sold on clearance? Was a marketing campaign from a social source paid or owned (meaning non-paid)? There are easily a hundred points of context behind most data sets that are missing. This is why landing unprocessed data in a fast analysis system does not necessarily yield massive insights. But do not panic. More data is not necessarily better, because correlation is not causation.

To use a fun analogy, the data problem faced by companies in the Listening Zone is like a wardrobe malfunction. The belt does not match the shoes, the shirt is all wrong, and what is with that hat? But at least Learners have the clothes to step outside. Listeners in the previous stage are missing their pants completely.

How Data Structure Holds Learners Back

The common practices that block or at least slow down a customer-centric transformation in the Learner stage are:

1. *We have tons of data but not enough insight!* When terabytes of big data are filling up storage servers daily, it can be hard for executives to understand why the insight is missing. This comes back to inconsistent data (also called "data governance") and missing context. It can be helpful to remember that data is fragile and contains no natural intelligence.

2. *We need to break down our data silos!* Yes, this is true, with a caveat. If a company established solid governance and use cases in the Listening Zone, then they now have a unique opportunity to create a competitive advantage by improving the quality of data. Pushing plain data together will not yield high-quality insights later but augmenting the data with better context will.

3. *We need to be more customer-centric!* I love it when companies start saying this, but due to challenges in the data, this often takes the form of great "customer experience" for all. There are many worthwhile ways to improve the overall customer experience, but true customer-centricity with bottom-line impact means you can individually identify who is a good customer and who is not

and offer different experiences accordingly. Leadership in the early part of the Learning Zone may not understand the financial impact of customer-centric data, but they clearly understand it by the time they exit.

One example of true customer-centric thinking is American Airlines "eagles" or Helix Score, a secret passenger scoring system that will determine the value of a customer. The airline found they could arm their frontline agents with this great decision-making tool so they could more easily extend offers, waive change fees, or offer upgrades. The system serves to identify valuable, but vulnerable customers. You cannot call American and ask for your score, nor would it do you much good because this dynamic system updates daily. Here's how it works: The agent sees up to five "eagles," which appear on the customer record. More eagles are correlated to customer loyalty and lifetime value but also to the competitiveness of your home city and the amount of inconvenience you might have experienced recently in delayed or canceled flights. Instead of showing more eagles for the customers who flew the most, the company developed this more sensitive measure. As a result, the frontline agents were armed with better information about when to bend the rules. Your eagle score probably won't get you an upgrade ahead of other passengers at the gate, but it could be the sweet difference between paying for change fees or not or earning bonus miles out of the blue.

By contrast, Wells Fargo bankers see a similar note on their screens indicating a "high value customer" is present. However, the resulting action is not to offer a special product or service tailored just to them, but to push more products. Wells Fargo's sales goals were so aggressive they led to Wells Fargo's agents to sell products that were unneeded, unused, and through the creation of fake accounts, unauthorized. According to a report in *USA Today*, the SEC found that, "Wells Fargo repeatedly misled investors, including through a misleading performance metric, about what it claimed to be the cornerstone of its Community Bank business model and its ability to grow revenue and earnings." Investors sued for fraud and ultimately Wells Fargo was forced to pay a $3 billon class-action settlement, of which $500 million went directly back to investors.

Could Wells Fargo have used American's Helix score to better serve vulnerable customers instead of a straight-line CLV calculation of customer value applied to product sales? Possibly, but data is still simply a tool of the executives who wield it. Executives with a customer-centric mindset would consider how the customer benefits before how the company benefits.

Why Learners Need Customer Lifetime Value

As companies enter the Learning Zone, they are not thinking about the value of each customer initially. If we think about customer-centric maturity as three stages of measurement, then the first part from the end of the Listening Zone is measuring volume and then the conversion from that volume. The second part is thinking about the general person or segment behind that conversion. But the third part has the most value for customer-centric transformation, and that is measuring the specific value of that unique customer (the unlocked revenue potential of CLV, which you first read about in the introduction).

When we add CLV, we shift from descriptive measures of the past into predictive metrics because CLV projects all future revenue dollars. CLV supports the overall measurement of customer equity which tells us the quality of the customer base, and by correlation, the quality of the business. Finally, CLV creates the bridge between customer touchpoints and bottom-line business value. CLV is what I call a "North Star" metric for every consumer-facing business.[3]

While the CLV formula should be customized to each business, let's take apart the fundamental features to see why this metric is so powerful. See Figure 4-1.

CLV is the sum of each individual customer's future purchases projected forward in time, minus all variable profits and costs (including acquisition costs) then discounted for the time value of money. To determine if a

• • •

3   CLV formulas work for B2B and B2B2C businesses as well, but the approach takes more care due to the heavy lumpiness of transactions and groupings of customer types which may not be mutually exclusive.

FIGURE 4-1

One Version of CLV Formula

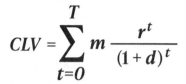

$$CLV = \sum_{t=0}^{T} m \, \frac{r^t}{(1+d)^t}$$

m is the net cash flow per period (while the customer is still "alive")
r is the rentention rate
d is the discount rate
T is the time horizon for the calculation

company is truly healthy from its customer base, we need to look beyond raw sales, because sales alone do not create company value. Profit (sales minus costs) creates company value. Why should we care about company value? Because when companies are resilient, they are not reliant on outside capital to fund their operations which allows them to focus, remain engaged, and project a deep sense of "heart" through their business. Then, when additional capital is needed, it is surgically applied to improve the business, not cover up expensive acquisition mistakes or generally push more product to the wrong customers via discounting.

CLV is often confused with Historical Value (based on Recency, Frequency, Monetary Value or "RFM") which calculates customer transactional history, minus costs, through today. CLV includes this history to fit the accuracy of the model, then projects beyond today into the future. The number of years we project forward varies according to the purpose, but common limits are 1 year, 2 years, 5 years, or 15 years, which is akin to infinity. The shorter the projection, the less uncertainty there is in the estimate, but the longer the projection, the more the total value of the customer is included, and the larger the overall customer equity number.

CLV asks: based on all prior transactions from this customer, what is the propensity of how much they might spend in the future? *Propensity* is an odd word to non-analysts but think of it like a statistical guess. If I spent $100 twice before, what are the odds I'll spend $100 tomorrow? Once a purchase is made, the likelihood of repurchase continues to decline until another purchase is made, but it is never zero (from a statistical perspective). CLV is not actual dollars you will put in the bank—it's a projection of potential dollars.

The Fundamental Ingredients of CLV

Let's walk through the elements that make up CLV. The letter "m" in the formula stands for margin which can be a constant. This reflects how much profit we can expect after deducting for variable costs including those sales and marketing costs to acquire or retain customers per period. If we want to use CLV to estimate the upper bounds of acquisition spending, then these costs need to be excluded (otherwise you could calculate a boundary which was not profitable at any lifetime).

The letter **r to the t** in the formula is the *probability that the customer is alive* after t periods. Retention rates vary widely across industries from 63 percent in retail to 84 percent in professional services. If retention is low, say 20 percent, the company would lose 100 percent of customers acquired at year five. Retention is not a constant. Many companies make this an average and use the same number across multiple years which is incorrect because that would underestimate customer value and misclassify customers. It's more accurate to recalculate the rate monthly, quarterly, or at least annually. This also assumes revenue is booked at beginning of the period where "t" equals zero. In a subscription model, you would use the billing cycle so revenue might book monthly or annually.

The letter **d** in the formula stands for *discount rate* which is the time value of money. Dollars received today are worth more than tomorrow. This is a good place to align with your CFO and match any company standard in place.

The capital **T** in the formula stands for the *time horizon*. How far are you projecting forward? For most companies, at 15 years there is little difference from infinity. Depending on your application of CLV, you may want to pull the maximum value of your customer base, or you may want a shorter range that could be more certain.

Note that the CLV formula does not and cannot account for products you have not released and customers who have not yet purchased. It is a long-range projection of the value of your customers as they sit in your business today. That is why it is important to refresh it frequently. How frequently depends on 1) how quickly you act on information springing from this metric and 2) how often your business releases products.

The virtue of CLV is that is communicates a new level of measuring performance. For example, based on the CLV, you might assess there is a .043 likelihood that this individual customer would spend $556 of today's dollars in the future. That might classify the customer as "medium value" potential. By joining the financial likelihood of a purchase to a specific use case, we can know when important medium-value customers are "product confused" and we can trigger a timely response to rescue that valuable yet vulnerable customer.

Further, because customer interactions stretch across so many departments, the addition of CLV to the master data set could affect and align performance measures across the company. It can be tempting to identify CLV as a "holy grail" of measurement and run it into the boardroom at this point, but do not do it. Instead, spend the time opening the gates of customer learning by using CLV strategically. CLV is a powerful tool to make strategic decisions that keep a company healthy, but customers should never be seen as only a number. Experimentation helps you know more about the people behind all that wonderful potential.

Here are five early ways to use CLV strategically:

1. Segment the customer base by customer value to unpack performance. As the volume of data rises, the demand to measure performance increases. Use CLV as a long-term measure of customer quality (high, medium, low value) across every customer touchpoint.
2. Within marketing, for example, you can tie CLV to your marketing acquisition spend, commonly called the customer acquisition cost (CAC), to the CLV ratio. Now you can have a good argument for what to spend in each channel or even why your marketing budget deserves an increase. This is a useful application, but not a favorite of mine for two reasons. First, channels don't buy products, customers do, and I think this tends to shift the focus away from the actual customer. Second, CLV is a long-term

projection so tying it to short-term acquisition strategies is directional at best.

3. Cohort customers by the acquisition month, quarter, or year to see if your company continues to acquire high-quality customers or if the quality is dropping over time.

4. Use cases defined in the Listening Zone can be powered up with an anonymous hash ID (a string of 20+ numbers or alphanumeric code that form a temporary customer ID) on the website, which creates a hook to connect customers to previous behaviors, once identification is known (e.g., when a purchase is made). When a company adds CLV, it quickly becomes clear where valuable customers are getting frustrated.

5. When customer value is connected to behavior, your experiment strategies can be ranked according to the future dollars saved or even recaptured.

Why Learners Need Experimentation

In the same way reporting was a tool for change at the Listening Zone, experimentation is the critical tool for change at the Learning Zone. But first, what is the difference between a test and an experiment? Tests are used to show everything works fine before launch. The expectation is not to learn, but to show an assumed outcome will be true (i.e., the rocket will fire). Experiments, however, are used to expand what we know through a scientific process. Even a "failed" experiment can contain valuable learnings, and they often do. Testing is still widely used to refer to experimentation, and you will see that term often in the podcast interviews I include in this book.

When a company adopts experimentation, it initializes a continuous learning cycle around customers. The *customer-centric flywheel* that you first read about in Chapter 2 (that virtuous cycle of happy customers returning and bringing all their friends) applies here. Early changes tend to be low-risk and somewhat tactical. That's okay because we do not learn to drive by customer data in a day. Experimentation means the company is trying to act on the listening data in order to learn. Early-stage experiments are usually done to resolve friction in the customer journey or to optimize conversion. Later experiments can be anchored to CLV to help prioritize which experiment goes first.

Well-done experimentation requires a strategic framework and can include personalization, loyalty programs, acquisition programs and any kind of optimization. Every time we try something new, it is basically an experiment to see what will happen. Out of 10 tests, eight will fail (including those which have unclear results) but failure is still learning which is the point.

Experimentation not only requires a control to determine success, but it needs an organized plan. Once experiments catch on within a company, everyone will want to run one, and no one will want to give up on their good idea through a failed experiment. Something must be wrong in the data, right? This denial is called the Semmelweis reflex, which is the tendency to discount what does not fit within one's existing belief system. You can get ahead of this with a strategic plan for your experiments.

It is also possible to have 12 different segmentations running across five different tools spread across three departments. For example, paid search may have a segmentation, the brand marketing may have a segmentation, and there may be an email segmentation. Segmentation is good. It is how we unlock value from the data. However, segmentation that does not interlock has the potential of causing mass confusion and delays the customer-centric transformation in the same way siloed reporting did in the Listening Zone. A strategic plan can help.

Eight Steps to a Strategic Plan for Experiments

Every company has limited resources, and this is especially true for experiments. A strategic plan for experiments tracks all the ideas, prioritizes them, and records the result. Here is how it works:

1. *Assume you have limited resources.* This will require you to prioritize your experiments.
2. *Gather hypotheses.* Customer-centric experiments tend to be more powerful when they cross departments. If a cross-department

experiment goes forward, then use the "2-pizza team rule" to remain nimble.[4] Include data that illustrates the problem, if possible. This forms your baseline measurement for success. Clearly state what success looks like and what will be done if the experiment succeeds.

3. *Value each hypothesis.* There are two ways to do this. Companies new to the Learning Zone may want to start with conversion use cases and then back into the many elements touched on the path to conversion. For example, customers that abandon the cart did not click to calculate their shipping costs. Therefore, we could calculate the potential value of this experiment by adding up all the customers who did calculate their shipping costs and assess a one percent lift, an increase in potential sales. This is just a logical guess, but the valuation can illustrate the financial impact of an experiment. A second way to do this for more advanced Learners is to include CLV. For example, we know more medium-value customers abandon the cart than high-value customers. If we moved two percent of medium-value customers to high value by unblocking this point of friction, it would be worth $X to us. The difference in the first example is we are using historic numbers. In the second example, we are using CLV which could produce larger numbers because it accounts for the potential of all future purchases (subject to the time frame of the calculation).

4. *Evaluate promising hypotheses including the level of effort.* Do we have enough traffic/calls/interactions to get statistical significance in a reasonable time? Is there a seasonal effect which might affect the experiment? Six weeks or less is a good timeframe for new experiments. Can we do it technically? Do we have resources to create assets for the experiment? Who will you target and how? Does this experiment fit with other initiatives? This last question is to make sure the purpose for the experiment does not disappear

• • •

4 An Amazon philosophy which says the team should be no larger than what could be fed with two pizzas. The smaller the team, the better the collaboration. This is about 8 people or less.

while it runs. For example, there is a new payment type on your site that you want to improve, but another team has already decided to remove that payment type soon. This would be a fruitless experiment.

5. *Schedule the experiment for development.* In addition to including a clear control, check to be sure it is doing what you think it is doing before the experiment goes live. Then check again to ensure the experiment is not creating a negative customer experience.

6. *Monitor the experiment.* This includes multiple channels such as call center, online, service agents. Are people having weird experiences?

7. *Analyze the results.* Significance is reached and the experiment has a winner—or more likely, it is inconclusive. Fight the urge to simply run it again. Let the analysts dig in to understand confounding results and extract learnings. Then, either release the winner or adjust and go back to step one.

8. *Socialize the knowledge.* This is the hook that supports the evolution of customer-centric business culture. To move through the Learning Zone, a company must be able to absorb and eventually build upon each customer insight. Socializing what you have learned already can also prevent repetitive experiments. Knowledge libraries are helpful here, but the best socialization is an executive shout-out.

When Learners begin this process, they may want to operate linear experiments, each one running after the other. That works out to approximately eight experiments a year. As it becomes clear that results are not always earth-shaking, the desire to run more experiments faster will increase. At this point, it is wise to add a project manager to coordinate the many aspects of experimentation.

What About Machine Learning and Artificial Intelligence?

When companies enter the Learning Zone, early applications of machine learning (ML) and artificial intelligence (AI) typically come through external tools. For example, an email tool might also suggest the best time of day to send the email, or whether a different headline will generate more opens. As the company increases their maturity, they (or an outside vendor) may add new algorithms to support narrow decision making like *prospect scoring* (identifying high-conversion behaviors) or *customer profile clusters* (identifying groups of customers who tend to act in a specific way such as first-time buyers). These are all great innovations if they can track to measurable, bottom-line performance.

At one company, a lengthy customer profiling effort was made using U.S. demographic and psychographic data. The company received seven customer personas including how much they would spend, age range, sex, and what their motivations were. When the CEO asked, "How many of these individuals are in our customer base already?" there was no way to connect them. This was not a good way to learn more about their customers or the unlocked future revenue they contained. In the Learning Zone, there is finally an internal appetite to drive by the data. By building a firm customer-centric point of view about how (and who) will take action on that data, you can avoid stray projects and maintain focus on building up healthier, happier customers over time.

Why Learners Need Urgency to Succeed

In the Learning Zone, data leadership appears sporadically. Perhaps your chief analytics officer (CAO) doesn't cover all the parts of the organization, and they report to a technology leader or a marketing leader. Or maybe you have a new chief data officer, but their role is not clear between the CIO and the CMO. Or maybe you really understand what should be happening, but you are at the director level, reporting to a VP who reports to a C-level person. It is difficult to get customer centricity to extend across the full organization in the Learning Zone, but you can still rack up a few quick wins as we've discussed in the CLV section.

If we cannot share the vision of how beautiful it is to empower customers and how that benefits both the business and the customer in the long run, or if we cannot think of ourselves as being of service to the customer, then it is hard to fully execute a customer-centric transformation. How can we enhance or improve the lives of our customers if we cannot get that vision across internally? Why do this? The answer is that we do it because there's real value behind customer equity, and we get to customer equity through customer-centric thinking supported by customer-centric data.

As a customer-centric data leader, one thing you can control is the sense of urgency you project. Think about your customers, desperately trying to find what they need and maybe even give you money. Help them! How fast can you respond to test results? How easily do you share findings with other departments? How fast can you run a new analysis? From the dynamic flow of your trended data to the timing of your stand-up meetings, urgency drives the flywheel.

Not every business has to be running at a daily or an intraday pace, but you do need to run at the speed of the customer. If your customers tend to research a lot before making their purchase (e.g., comparing decorative tile for a bathroom remodel) then maybe your sense of urgency starts as monthly and moves to weekly. But if your customer purchases quickly, almost as an impulse (e.g., glancing at new lipstick shades) and you really need to know what's happening right away, then start weekly and eventually move to daily. Moving too fast can burn out your team, so be sure you're ready to take action on the information you receive, which will still be imperfect. Either way, now is the time to start connecting customer behavior to customer value and start racking up those measurable wins.

Tactics to Transform Learners to Leaders

The transformation from Learner to Leader is all about initializing and then spinning the customer-centric flywheel of the business. As it begins to turn, there are lots of fits and starts. One brand or product line might move faster than another. Politics and turf wars may erupt internally as the power of customer data—and ultimately customer equity—becomes clear. The goal is to keep moving forward and gaining momentum. Listen to each other internally, build, and grow. Remember our story about Nike? Today, when you pull up Nike's investor page, it says in bold letters, "Nike is a Growth Company." That's not by accident.

Technology that Transforms Learners

As companies enter the Learning Zone, they may substitute digital tracking systems like Adobe or Google as their customer database. Gradually, the technology needs to put the wealth of the business in one place, at the grain of the customer. To do that, technology must identify the customer and match all interactions and behaviors to the customer. Speed and flexibility are fundamental needs. You may also want an analytics landing zone as you work out data sharing and security rules to be able to give data and get data. If you have multiple terabytes of data grinding through every day like a lot of major retailers do, then it is a time-consuming process to move that much data from one place to another. Analysis will only be able to run as fast as the data is available, so you may only be able to initially move at the weekly level when you need to move at the daily level. Build for speed and scale and get ahead of it. Data is not getting any slower or smaller.

Actions People take as Learners

As we enter the Learning Zone, we keep watching the data to see what's changing. The reports get bigger and deeper, and as experimentation takes off, non-analyst stakeholders are expected to take action on the data. This is when self-service tools emerge like Tableau dashboards, but adoption usually remains low. A good way to solve for low adoption is to train a handful of internal influencers.

Influencers are strong internal mentors across teams. In any company, they make up about five percent of employees. Influence does not track to title, but you know who these people are. They are the person who's always the first one to raise their hand to say, "I'll try that," or "I know how that works." And they seem to learn things as if they're just breathing air. Influencers trained on self-service data tools create a "seed" within the company culture that allows one person to lean over and ask their neighbor how to get a report instead of creating a backlog of service tickets for the analysis team. Visualizations improve. Live data appears on the wall and teams begin to use it to support decisions in meetings. Knowledge libraries form to document learnings from the experiments that are beginning to take root. And ultimately, data creates better compliance with standards. A sense of the future accountability takes hold.

You're now able to see data from other business units. It forms a "give to get" paradigm that encourages alignment and participation. You're able to start to use more predictive customer-centric data, which means more business value is attached to everyday activities because you're driving it back to actual dollar value change in the business. Finally, people feel less afraid to have personal goals tied to their ability to get data-driven recommendations moving.

Leadership for Executives in Learner Stage

Leadership is critical in the Learner stage both at the entry and exit points. That's why you see a lot of organizations adding a chief data officer (CDO), a chief analytics officer (CAO) or a combination of the two. Leaders should be learning who your good customers are and what they do in sales, marketing, business intelligence, finance, call center, and support and how much revenue they represent based on individually calculated (not averaged) lifetime value. We are not thinking about only the marketing department anymore. We're thinking about the holistic customer. Leaders are working hard to find those quick cross-department wins. There is usually some nice low-hanging fruit that once seen through the data, can be knocked out right away. These early data leaders must stretch across all departments, and these are highly political roles. They often work at making friends across the departments to gain alignment and get at least some boats rowing in the same direction.

Processes that Support Learners

The Learning Zone is a process-heavy time. At this point, we're looking at cross-business units and the more acceptable medium-risk experiments start to become tolerable. As the company progresses in customer-centric transformation, tolerance increases to try, learn, and sometimes fail. Business impact increases as customer-centric tests are tied to CLV. As a result, more optimizations (the result of a test) become internalized knowledge, and that knowledge begins to appear in business algorithms. To maintain the progress, Learners need to create and maintain a data dictionary including the source of record. Experimentation should be backed up by a knowledge library where previous tests and findings are recorded. Finally, a trackable list of tests including the expected amount of revenue and actual ROI they generated creates a nice insurance policy when the inevitable new executive questions whether customer-centric transformation is working.

Two more processes that will help you defend early momentum in this zone are the report rate and recommendation adoption rate. The *report rate* simply tracks how often reports are accessed and by whom. If reports are sent via email, a campaign code can be used to track this. If reports are accessible online, then simply drop in the out-of-the-box Google Analytics or Adobe Analytics page tracking script and capture the login ID, if possible. This process tells you how often reports (which actively support transformation) are accessed.

The *recommendation adoption rate* is a simple but powerful process. As new analytics recommendations are made (usually through extensive presentations), track each recommendation on a separate list and who is responsible for taking action. At the end of the year, you will be likely to have over 100 recommendations to point to that your team made, thereby validating the effort, and shifting the problem where it belongs—to the internal cultural expectation to act on customer-centric data.

Metrics for Learners

In the Learning Zone we monitor report and adoption rates, track data sources of record, and build a data dictionary to prevent companies from sliding back down the curve. These are defensive measures that protect your progress. Within existing dashboards or at least in context with experiments or analyses, we monitor customer voice and behavior, watch the flow of behavioral segments (including CLV) and message resonance as well as the customer acquisition cost (CAC) to CLV ratio to help expedite your progress. These are offensive measures that accelerate progress. See Figure 4-2.

Exit Criteria

The exit criteria for Learners are not only the technology but the internal attitude that this is the dawn of a new normal, and that takes a lot of executive leadership. Ask yourself:

FIGURE 4–2

What to Measure in Learning Zone

Measures That Protect	Measures That Accelerate
Listening Zone Still Applies	**Customer Voice/Survey + Behavior**
Report Rate	• Longitudinal
• Internal usage of reports	• Point or moment based
Recommendation Adoption Rate	**Segmentation Flow**
• Execution on recommendation	• Rising or Falling CLV segments
Data Source-of-Record	• External (e.g., share of wallet)
Data Dictionary	**Message Resonance**
	• Campaign code
	Cost
	• Customer acquisition cost to CLV

- *Is the organization aligned around the customer?* That means we're really looking at the lifetime value as a measure of performance quality.
- *Is the data at the individual grain of every customer?* Because just like you would connect with friends at a party, you want to speak to every person individually. You don't want to give them the same message or even cluster the same message; you really want to start to align around the individual nature of each customer.

When we use customer data effectively, we build customer equity and that's bottom-line value for your company.

CUSTOMER EQUITY ACCELERATOR INTERVIEW

How Naked Wines Became Customer-Centric with Greg Banbury, Cofounder of Naked Wines

Greg Banbury, cofounder of Naked Wines joined me on my podcast to discuss customer-centric growth. From loyal customers to employees to award-winning products, customer-centric success is woven into the culture of Naked Wines. As I interviewed Greg, I wondered what might make the culture at Naked Wines different? And where did they source their ideas for experimentation (testing)? Take a look at our conversation where Greg explained how his company innovates and sustains healthy growth driven by customer lifetime value.

Can you tell us a little bit more about Naked Wines and what your team is up to there?

Banbury: Sure, at Naked Wines, we are disrupting the wine industry by connecting the world's best winemakers with everyday wine drinkers for the benefit of our winemakers, customers, staff, and investors. We're a pure-play online subscription retailer. We now have over half a million "angel" customers worldwide, and we're producing over a thousand wines from 200 winemakers in 17 countries. And my team is responsible for driving growth here within the U.S. market.

It's interesting that you use the term angels because this is not just a wine club.

Banbury: That's right, yes. So, we're working directly with some of the world's most renowned independent winemakers, and through our platform, we are directly connecting them with our customers. And there's a funding element to all of this, which we can talk about as we go on. And that's why we call our customers "angels." Going back to the idea of angel funding, our customers can actually help the independent winemakers produce incredible wines in what you call a unique model that generates fantastic customer loyalty.

I see a lot of companies who seem to be acquiring as many customers as possible. They call that customer-centric, and then they shoot to have a big Wall Street exit. Is that customer-centric growth?

Banbury: Well, the tricky thing is that the only customers you're ever going to make any money from are the ones that stick around. We do that by delivering on our proposition of delivering delicious wines by directly connecting winemakers and wine drinkers. And I think we've all seen what can happen if you go too far and spend money like water without deploying capital in a responsible way, WeWork being the most recent example of that. Our team has a complete obsession about making things better for our customers and our winemakers, really with that focus on loyalty and customer lifetime value. When we started the business, it was simple: wine made by a real person and not wine made in a factory will taste better. And we also knew that winemakers were more like artists and given creative freedom and funding, they can focus on their products.

They would make world-class wines without the price tag. And we know that there's not a bottle of wine in the world that costs more than $20 to make. If you're ever paying more than $40 for wine that you're drinking at home, not in a restaurant, obviously, you're paying for things that you simply cannot taste. Once we knew how to access these incredible wines from these huge and talented winemakers, the next question was, "Okay, well, how will we fund them?" And some bright spots in the team suggested, "Well, why don't we ask our customers?" And that's what we do.

Our customers, who we already touched on, we call them angels. They prepay us. They put money into the Naked Wines accounts so that we can commission the best winemakers in the world to make wines exclusively for them. And when the wine is ready, the customers who helped us get exclusive access to those wines. That's sort of a wholesale price. We're really driving consumer customer loyalty through a great product. And essentially, what we've done is create a virtuous circle where the winemaker is liberated to focus on making a great product. And because the wine tastes great, the customers stick around, and because they stick around, we're able to invest more in winemakers and more in growth.

You're not like a lot of companies who will discount for loyalty, put everything on sale, and call that loyalty. In your case, you're using community and emotion to drive that virtuous circle. Is that right?
Banbury: That's right. And when we first started thinking about the business, as I said at the start, we knew we were only ever going to make money (and remember that the point is to make some money) from the customers that stick around. For us, loyalty is a feeling. It's

not a program. And so how were we going to generate that feeling from our customers? We felt it when we were speaking to the winemakers. They're incredibly passionate people.

I believe the term "angel investor" came from Broadway in New York. People were writing plays and shows that would never have seen the light of day if it weren't for people getting involved and putting up the cash to make these shows possible. And that's exactly the kind of emotional connection we've now got from connecting our everyday wine, drinking customers, getting them nice and close to the passionate artists who make just the most incredibly delicious wines.

And that's not a typical retail relationship. These days, people like to know where their product is coming from, and they like to know that it's an authentic product. They like to know that nobody is losing out in the process, that it's a sustainable model at play. And ultimately, what we've ended up with at Naked Wines is an incredibly vibrant community. Like any good community, they help each other out when times are tough, they grow together and improve as time goes by. And the output for us as a business is incredibly loyal customers.

How do you know that the loyalty is there? Because CLV, for example, will give you a lot of transactive information, but it won't give you that sense of community, and it seems like if I'm right, you might be coupling the two together. You see the transactional stream, but you also see the qualitative information coming back from the comments. Is that a fair assumption?

Banbury: It is, yeah. I mean, there's a whole bunch of things that go into the way that we look at customer lifetime value. And a number of those things are to do with engagement and engagement outside of purchasing. And if you have a business that has multiple touchpoints with your customer, then you really need to understand all those factors that go into customer lifetime modeling because you will quite quickly see that an engaged customer will buy more in the long run anyway. If you really focus on the customer experience and as I said, we tend to obsess about what the experience is like for our customers, not just from a physical wine product perspective, but also technology, customer service, that all those different things that go into producing our customer lifetime value. That really is key to having a truly customer-centric business.

Are there some examples that you can share about the decisions with the formula or with the company and cultural aspect that go along the path of sustaining customer-centric growth?
Banbury: Definitely. I think that having a "test and learn" culture is critical so that you can grow your investment in new customers aggressively, but without having to bet the ranch. I think I've already mentioned that we love to make things better for our customers. And the way we do that is by extensively testing across all aspects of the customer life cycle. And sure, some will impact the very, very top of the funnel so that we can grow faster, but others will improve that long tail of customer lifetime value, which means that you can afford to spend more to acquire that same customer. But both the improvements at the top of the funnel and the improvements to customer lifetime value, both drive growth. And I think that for us, a shift to quality over quantity, that is a big point to make.

I love that you said that. I just cannot tell you how many businesses have not figured that out yet.
Banbury: I mean if you ever want to make any money, you need to have a disciplined approach to investing in growth. And for us, we have a target, and I have a minimum four times payback over the customer's lifetime. When that payback, when that target is met, we will invest aggressively and where it isn't, we will free up capital for investment elsewhere. So, what that might translate into are fewer but better customers. And those better customers will stick around for longer, and you will make more money from them. You end up opening more opportunities for growth because those valuable customers mean that your allowable cost to acquire more goes up as well. And we have one rule internally with optimization—and this is

a cultural point—we don't debate, we prototype. And so essentially there is no such thing as a bad idea. As long as you can build proof of concept and make it measurable, we'll put it in front of our customers, and we will let data lead the discussion, not a committee of people sitting around a meeting table saying, "I think this will work." You have to let data be the guide.

And yet I've seen so many people who say, "Oh well, we do testing; we have the red button or the blue button." But that's not the internal culture of testing, which is what you just explained is taking disagreements, prototyping them, seeing what wins, and letting the customers decide.

Banbury: That's exactly right. And you know, we've had some crazy ideas tabled in the past that I think if they were to have been debated, would have never seen the light of day. But we prototype those tests. We put them in front of customers and absolutely let the data be.

Are there any crazy ideas you want to share?

Banbury: Yeah, so we very recently launched market pricing on our wines. This was a test to prove the value of the product to our angels because the wines are being exclusively commissioned for our customers. It was important to us that the pricing on the wines is authentic. What we tested was if we show our customers a similar wine in the marketplace and actually linked to that product on a competitor's website and show the price of that product, do we see a win to customer lifetime value? And that seems like a crazy test, right? Why on earth would we link to the competitors' website, but the test won and now on every single one of our wines, you will see a benchmark price, which we call the market price, where the wine has been blind tasted against these other wines that are available in the market. You can see exactly how much they cost. The result is customers see the authenticity in the product, and the value proposition resonates even further. So yeah, that was a crazy one when it was first tabled, but it's one that now is a really important part of our customer proposition.

Does that translate across cultures? Like I know in the U.S. culture, we have this embedded idea that it must cost more in order for it to taste good.

Banbury: I think there's definitely some learning that we can share with our customers. Certainly around exactly how much it costs to make a bottle of wine. And you would be amazed at a typical $20 bottle of wine, how much money is going in the juice versus things that you can actually taste. We flip that around by saying we work "open book" with our winemakers and when they need the funds to pay the grower for the fruit, we know all the component parts that make up that cost of the bottle. And if you are one of our angels and you're able to help us fund that wine, make that wine possible, then you effectively pay a price that is very much close to the component parts of that wine. Whatever it comes out is what you pay. And we will benchmark taste that wine against similar wines in the market, as I've said. We've cut out all the costs that you cannot taste, and you really can get a phenomenal wine for under 25 bucks. And that is something that our angels and certainly our existing customers in the U.S. have tapped into and something that they're really enjoying and finding valuable. And that's why they stick around.

We test extensively through the customer lifetime cycle, and that means the important part is onboarding you in the right way. The benefit of having long-term profitable customers is that you can spend money to recruit those customers. We will put a very good offer in front of you for your first time with us because we want you to try the product and the benefit to you as a customer. You know that we're going to put our best foot forward in that case because we were not going to make any money from you unless you come back, so we're prepared to lose money on that first order because we want you to experience not just how good these winemakers are, but also the customer service. We have a phenomenal home delivery network across the United States delivering usually within two days to most of the major cities. From there, it's an experiential thing.

You download our mobile app that you can scan the label to rate the wine, see a video of the winemaker, and all this stuff starts to make clear that you are part of something that's more than just a retail experience. It is something that you can become as involved in or, if not, as you wish. Some people sit on the sidelines and don't rate their wines and still get a fantastic experience because they enjoy the products. But others, you know that they're on the website daily chatting with other angels and hearing what's going on with directly from the winemakers when they're in the winery or in the vineyard. And it's just a wonderful community.

Did you see the mobile app become a way to drastically increase the engagement of the community? I don't know if you always had that, but it seems like it might've been something that you added as you went.
Banbury: Yeah, I know, I mean back in 2008 when we launched, it was this idea of crowdfunding and the social network was still new, but nowadays obviously it's the norm. And so yes, we built a mobile app initially for our customers to be able to make those small interactions that we want to do immediately. Like read about the wine, watch a little video of the winemaker, and give feedback on the quality of the wine. We built all of those into the mobile app. And then we built an app just for those 200 people, those winemakers, so our winemakers have a mobile app as well they can use it to post content directly to their customers. When you're stuck behind a desk in an office in the city, of course, you want to be transported to the beautiful countryside and see exactly where your money is going. When you do sit down that evening to open your bottle of Matt Parish cabernet, you feel like that connection to him is real. So yeah, technology has been a big part of cultivating lifetime value from our customers, but we do it in a very customer-focused way. How can we make the experience better for the customer? Technology has definitely helped us do that.

You say a phrase like, "We look for ways to make the technology better for the customer," but I think what's really happening underneath, especially when you talk about testing and CLV is you're not treating all customers as one bucket. There is a lot of heterogeneity in the base

as you understand different segments of customers, different ways that
they are interacting with you. And it strikes me that through the mobile
app, especially, you're able to understand individuals and their quality
of engagement and relate that back to the purchase streams. Whereas
a website that didn't have a mobile app would have to rely on people
logging in or some other kind of cookie methodology to pull people
together and understand that. So, I think this is actually a strong piece
to get your CLV vision together and see what's driving it. Is that fair?
Banbury: Yeah. Look, and I think whatever tool it is, whether it's
a mobile app or you have stores, and you're collecting data that
way is all about understanding your customers and gathering as
much information on their behavior that you can to understand the
different segments to try and drive the behaviors that you know
lead to a better experience for your customers. We know who has
the mobile app. We know who doesn't. Let's try rather than sending
this person an email to buy this week, send them an email to get
them to download the app. Foregoing short-term sales for long-
term loyalty is something that we constantly think about when
we're communicating with our customers and looking at the way we
segment the base.

That makes a lot of sense. We've always had this discussion internally
about behavior versus demographics, and my opinion has largely
been that you can have identical demographics but radically different
behavior, and it's the behavior that's predictive. Is that what you found
as you relate it to customer lifetime value? That the behavior is really the
driver of CLV?
Banbury: There's definitely some demographic data that will go into
the modeling, but absolutely, the big drivers are that we look for
behavioral changes, and we will group people together who looked
like they're behaving in the same way as opposed to just defining
them as objects that don't move (like your location). It's very much
about how you're interacting about the actions that you're taking as
opposed to the information that you tell us about yourself in terms
of where you are or how old you are. You've got to look at all this

behavioral data. If you've got it, and if you don't have it, then you need to find a way to get it because it really is the key because you can then try and change behavior if you're tracking it.

I love that answer because it's so closely related to who we are as people—not just a transaction and not just an age, ZIP code, and other demographic information. I think what we do is so critical. You talk about quality of customer over quantity and there's been some pressure in some companies, particularly smaller companies where investors will come in. They'll say, "Well, you know, it's great that you've tapped into this particular tribe, but we really want you to prove that you're not a niche and that you can play in all these other spaces." And yet a counterargument I've heard to that is that when a brand stays close to its niche and its customers, they can go deeper within that group instead of spreading out laterally. Is there a balance between going deep and going wide, or is there some way that customer lifetime value and being customer-centric can guide you in that decision?

Banbury: I think the guiding principle always has to be if you ever want to make money from your customers, then you need to understand customer lifetime value and you should be focusing on retaining those customers for as long as possible. And certainly, for us, understanding customer lifetime value and everything that goes into it is our guiding principle. We were never going to go on a land grab of customers if they weren't going to deliver that lifetime value because otherwise, we would have been poor custodians of the capital that we had to allocate on behalf of our investors. My answer would be no, we want to grow in a sustainable way. And I'm sure that there are obviously going to be companies out there with different objectives, but for us, it was about building a sustainable business. I said at the start we wanted to revolutionize the wine industry, and you can't do that if you are here today, gone tomorrow. And we want to be making long-term commitments to our winemakers so that their livelihoods are changed, and the impact ripples through the growing community of fruit growers and the surrounding communities because of it. I mean, that's where meaningful change comes from. For us, it was always about the long game. But I understand that there will be other businesses with other objectives. You just need to decide which one you're in. And if you're in the lifetime value game, then it's all about making things better for your customers.

It sounds like if you're going deep into a space that there's still a lot of space for innovation.
Banbury: Oh, absolutely. Like I said, despite being six, seven years old in the U.S. market now, we're constantly challenging ourselves to come up with new ways of looking at things. The pricing model that I described earlier is just one of those ways. Innovation should never stop. If you stand still, eventually someone's going to catch you. So you must focus on that continuous improvement cycle, which is where the "test and learn" comes in. And if someone's got an idea on how to do it better, we will never reject it, and we'll see what the data tells us. But innovation must be a key part of your culture to keep that energy on improving the customer experience.

Let's say I'm convinced, and you know I love the way your business is operating and how it is truly customer-centric. What should I do if I want to get my company to be more truly, sustainably customer-centric? What should I do first?
Banbury: I think you need to have a good look at the customer lifetime and try and work out all the drivers of customer lifetime value, which is obviously a data exercise. And by far, the biggest driver in customer lifetime value would be retention. What can you do to improve the customer experience? They do stick around for longer. And is that investing in product quality? Is it investing in your people internally, your team, and your culture? Is it customer service, is it technology? And then I think, you know, have a culture of transparency. As business leaders, we know that transparency is a critical part of team culture, but it also extends to your customers and your suppliers. Transparency builds trust and, therefore, loyalty. A good example of that, as I said, is the transparent market pricing

that we launched. And the one step further on that pricing is that if our customers seem to disagree with the pricing based on their ratings, then we drop the price on the wine. We have customer-powered pricing on our high end as well.

Is that right?
Banbury: Absolutely, yes. So, the wine doesn't stack up every six months. We review the price, and we'll drop the prices if the customers agree it's at the right spot. And all of that came about because of our "test and learn" culture. I guess the final point would be no idea is a bad idea. If you can prototype it and get it in front of customers, don't sit around the table for hours debating it. You'll only kill what could potentially be a game-changing idea and then let the data guide you.

Am I right in thinking that your ideas can come from anywhere in the organization? It's not like there's one team that sits in a room.
Banbury: Yes. Some of the best ideas have come from the guys in our call center or even winemakers. We encourage that innovation to come from all facets of the business. And yeah, like I said, no idea is a bad idea. Everybody's opinion counts if you're accountable to your idea. So, we don't just have a free-for-all. You have to be able to state your objective and then obviously let the data prove or disprove that objective. If you don't know how to do that, we have someone in the business that will help you frame up what the objective and what the measurable might be. But no, absolutely ideas can come from any part of the organization. I think we have a Google form that allows people from any part of the businesses to submit their ideas and they get reviewed on a regular basis. So no, it's very much part of the culture that everyone can submit an idea. And like I said, some of the craziest, wackiest ideas have ended up being the best.

The way that your company is operating is tight model for the 21st-century corporation where you've broken down the walls or between a corporation and the customer, and you've allowed the customers to lead the business but not lead it in a willy-nilly fashion. You're basically the arbiter of the information coming back and the arbiter of the community. Kudos to your team and all the people at Naked Wines who have contributed to this modern thinking in this process. It is not simple to do, and it is something that I think you've done a great job of, just following your instincts, and really following your heart to create a wonderful platform for bringing these audiences together.

Banbury: That's very kind, and you touched on it there, but really, we do have a phenomenal team of people across the UK, Australia, and the U.S. and we've talked a little bit about the team culture. But you know, many, many great ideas have failed with a poorly put together team. We're very fortunate to have a wonderful group of people who are all behind our purpose of connecting winemakers to wine drinkers. And that extends fortunately for us through our team to our winemakers and to our staff who I believe everyone feels like they're a part of the Naked Wines story.

At Naked Wines, the "test and learn" process fueled their understanding of customers. Further, ideas for these experiments could come from anywhere in the company in a quest to better serve their customers. They also benefit from a mobile app that provides additional value to their customers while also improving customer-centric insights especially as the company looked to establish a sense of community and emotional loyalty. As a company moves from the Learning to the Leadership Zone, customer-centric thinking takes root with senior management and new financial metrics align profit with customer benefit.

• • •

CUSTOMER-CENTRIC TAKEAWAYS

- **With trusted data and a history of taking reasonable low-risk actions, Learners create a culture that values experimentation and can confidently move forward with medium-risk actions.**

→ A key concept at this stage is changing the basis of measurement to customer value via properly calculated CLV.

→ There should be an increasing sense of urgency around the C-level which supports increasing investments in technology, data science, people, and the processes that maintain progress.

→ Late in the Learning Zone is a good time to bring on a CAO, CDO, or other senior specialist data leader, if that talent is not already part of the management team.

CHAPTER 5

Zone 3: Leading With Customer Data

DOES THIS sound like your company?

Electronic Arts (EA) was founded in 1982 by former Apple employee Trip Hawkins and quickly became a pioneer of early home computer games. Hawkins wanted to sell directly to consumers from the start, but the company was releasing relatively unknown game brands, which made sales challenging. In late 1984, Larry Probst arrived as VP of Sales and changed the strategy to retail distribution, which improved EA margins and increased awareness. In 1991, Hawkins stepped down as CEO and Probst took over. EA began producing console games for Nintendo in 1990 and later Sony PlayStation in 1995, as well as Hawkin's new company console 3DO. EA continued to expand through the 1990s and into the early 2000s driven in part by the acquisition of dozens of game design studios as well as exclusive content licensing deals with NFL, ESPN, and the CLC for college football content. EA was the first game publisher to release annual updates of its games (including fresh team rosters) and make them available across all game platforms. In 2007, Probst stepped down and passed the reigns internally to John Riccitiello, who was also a passionate gamer. Riccitiello took more care to maintain the independence of small game studios once acquired. He reorganized the company into a city-state model where each of its four core labels were responsible for its own product development and publishing. Now a multinational brand, EA was a company 10,000 employees-strong with pressure to get quality games to market faster.

Zachery Anderson joined EA late in 2007 as a *demand planner*, a person who forecasts revenue to align inventory levels. He spent 12 years at Electronic Arts leading the customer-centric transformation to "Player First" thinking as SVP and chief analytics officer. In 2020, he left to explore new challenges with Royal Bank of Scotland's NatWest Group. He knows calculating CLV is not the same as acting on it.

With a deep background in economics and a desire to understand human behavior, Zack immediately noticed EA had a lot more data than they knew what to do with. If that data could be used correctly, Zack knew he could help the company see customer behavior, make better games, and ultimately make better financial decisions. But EA was still heavily sales-distribution focused, striving to get discs into stores like Walmart, Target, Best Buy and in Europe, Carrefour. The company was starting to shift to a sell-through focus where EA used its marketing powerhouse to drive customer demand which would, in turn, sell product off retail shelves. All the data coming back to the company was aggregated product sales, so Zack only had the timing of sales to work with initially. The timing told him most EA products sold heavily in the first week of release, and then experienced a 70-percent drop as sales trickled along thereafter. But Zack wanted to know more about the individual players. Was it the same players from one game to the next, or different ones? How much did they play the game? Luckily, the first online consoles, the Xbox 360 and PlayStation 3, were just coming out, and with them, a stream of individual player registration data. Zack pitched EA's management team to run a special project to analyze this data, and they approved it. Zack and one other person dug in and discovered, that yes, all the players who registered the game in the first week were the same as those who registered in the first week the previous year. It was EA's first taste of individual, heterogenous customer data.

Zack's initial data sets from 2006, 2007, and 2008 were small. They certainly did not include every EA customer. But the finding was huge. Not only did the players come back year after year, but whether they came back was based on how much they played the previous game. If a player bought Madden NFL and played it for 100 hours, the chance they would buy the next year's game was extremely high. Zack realized the players did this because it's enjoyable. This customer-centric revelation really transformed the way EA thought about the business.

Up until this point, EA made games as products. They marketed them, pushed them out, and then it was done. They realized they were running more of a non-contractual subscription service with the annual release of sports games. Further, the product investment and engagement with players over the long term of the game, not just the first week, would be required to increase player retention and ultimately make the company grow. Zack thought, "Wow. This is how we increase our customer lifetime value—by building games that people enjoy for longer and can engage with for longer and then their likelihood to buy the next game goes up."

But then, the world entered the financial crisis of 2008 when the housing market bubble burst and banks who had taken too much risk began to fail. EA's sales were already slowing and with a huge portfolio of games; it began to shut down studios and laid off 11 percent of its workforce. At the time, EA was spending 22 percent of revenue on marketing and sales and not enough was going into making great games. Marketing was a hot place to strike first, and it was something Zack knew the company had to fix.

And so, Zack focused all his team's energy on marketing. He delivered models and new principles. At the time, EA's marketing focused on huge audiences but low targetability. Zack wanted to encourage the marketing department to use their dollars to find people who would be likely to play the games for a long time (otherwise known as high-value customers). It wasn't a new concept for marketing, but CLV gave his team the tool to actualize it. To use CLV, EA couldn't share all that data with an external agency, so they had to build up their own internal media strategy group. Zack helped build a bunch of new systems that started bringing marketing cost down dramatically. As a percentage of revenue, marketing and sales costs dropped from 22 percent to below 12 percent, which means hundreds of millions of dollars were now dropping to the bottom line and available to be invested back into the product.

In 2013, EA got a new CEO, Andrew Wilson. One of the first moves Wilson made was to shift one of the core pillars of the company to player-first customer-centricity. And he backed it up when he told Wall Street the primary metric the company would run by would no longer be top-line sales. Wilson invested in Zack's analytics and data science group to help facilitate the new leadership strategy. As a result, Zack's team immediately got to work improving products.

EA already had a product in market called *Battlefield 4*. They were about to launch a prequel called *Battlefield 1*. With analytics in hand, the company made a bold decision to aggressively support the current in-market product *Battlefield 4*. This was counter-intuitive to the typical approach of ramping down investment in the old game as the new game comes to market.

Zack's team began a year ahead of the launch by investing in building new levels to the game, more content for the game, and they fixed things that were not working well all with the goal that they would boost player engagement. In the process, EA learned a lot about what they would need to put into the next game, *Battlefield 1*. In other words, Zack says, "It was this great virtuous cycle. We drove up engagement activity, which brought in a lot of new customers at the end of the *Battlefield 4* period to then hopefully move them over to *Battlefield 1*." The launch of *Battlefield 1* was the biggest launch EA has ever produced. It was the number-one selling game in the U.S. and sold more units globally than any game of its type. It was a huge success. Electronic Arts stock reached an all-time high with a value of $148.73 in July of 2018. *Battlefield 1* was released in October 2016.

Zack connected data, analysis, and CLV projects to real outcomes and the right questions. He says, "We started on marketing, which at the time was a crucial thing for the company to figure out and that helped a lot, that built our credibility, that had a big impact on the company that made the company willing to invest in the analytics and customer data space and then you know, very quickly we transitioned to another big key driver which is which products to make and what should be in those products."

Zack also cites the need to build your own data capital and invest the time to think about how you're going to use that. This is not something that can be outsourced. You need your own technologies, tools, and data science team. Then think systematically about how to scale and support a high volume of decisions early.

Although Zack was not a senior executive at the time, he thought like one. His view was the whole company. He says, "If you think company-wide and customer-first, the employees begin to think as one organization. We still get it wrong at times for sure, but I think the benefit for the company has been a huge turnaround and a lot happier customers for us."

He goes on to say, "The funny thing about even just the basics of calculating CLV crosses boundaries. So, I had to interact with our sales organizations or marketing organizations or product organization, our finance organization. And if I had stuck in one of those silos, we would never have the impact of this thinking." To drive change, you must be willing to cross boundaries, and that is where executive support of your legitimacy is critically important.

In this chapter you will learn the common traits of companies in the Leadership Zone, why CLV analysis can be a tool for transformation, how to get budget for data science projects, how to think about competitor's imitations and several ways to lead a data-driven customer-centric culture. At the end, I'll review specific tactics related to technology, processes, leadership, people, and metrics.

Common Traits of Companies as they Enter the Leadership Zone

As you can see in the EA example, Zack's timing and ability to get the ear of the new CEO did a lot to move the company through the Learning Zone and into the Leadership Zone. Here are some traits you can see in companies that are becoming Leaders:

- There is a deep sense of value in data and an urgent desire to use it.
- Technologies that allow executives to hear each customer's digital signal are in place.

- When quality analysis uproots the norm, the CEO takes an active interest.
- Leaders are constantly held accountable for taking action on data and as a result, the definitions behind the metrics are not up for debate.
- Because data science and experiments may still leave us with questions, innovation often occurs around novel and precise ways to understand customer desires.
- Supporting processes are consistent and, whenever possible, automated.

If this sounds like your company, you are probably leading the pack. The process to becoming even more customer-centric can be expedited by filling any gaps and taking the right steps, particularly around the financial and social alignment of doing right by the customer.

Here are five more ways to use CLV strategically:

1. EA had game telemetry to analyze (where any user was within the game at a specific time). By using CLV, the analysts were able to prioritize which parts of the game were more urgent to fix. This could include making it easier or harder to please the right customers. You can apply this type of analytic approach to identify priorities.
2. CLV can also be used in conjunction with geography including country, state, designated market area (DMA), or ZIP code level to understand where the customer base shows the most promise. This can be a good way to identify promising locations for pop-up shops or even physical stores.
3. The application of CLV against the product portfolio can show trends that would otherwise be hidden. For example, by volume, a product may appear to have lackluster sales. But when paired with CLV, we can see most purchases of the product are by high-value customers. This indicates a more valuable anchor product than originally assumed.

4. Similarly, when product margin is paired with CLV, it quickly becomes clear which products should receive more promotion (high margin, low CLV) or completely reconsidered (low margin, low CLV).

5. When front line agents are connected to CLV trends, it can allow expanded options to further empower these agents.

How Resistance to Change Holds Leaders Back

As access to data increases in speed and multiple departments are contributing to the same knowledge sharing system for insights and optimizations, your company may feel it is not able to respond fast enough. One solution is to shift to customer teams for faster execution. You should only consider this option once customer data and test optimizations are flowing fast. This might begin as a matrix shift and then move into a full-blown reorganization around the customer for the sheer need of speed. The measure of success in either case is knowing whether the organization can execute customer-centric decisions faster.

Most executives leading a customer-centric change underestimate the logistics and time it takes for change to take root. It is compelling to believe that once this revolutionary idea is shared, everyone will follow. Early Leaders do find pockets of acceleration where perhaps one internal team has more to gain or is already data savvy. It is the combination of knowledge sharing plus the ability to take action plus organizational alignment that is like the grease in the wheels of a customer-centric transformation. Internally, people feel they have the authority and the obligation to support a customer-first mentality. Not aligning to the customer within the organization will eventually stall customer-centric transformation progress. When you do reach that internal alignment, the conversation typically turns to the issue of funding.

Once a company begins to see traction in customer analytics, the natural response is to believe project funding will easily follow. However, that is not always the case. The successful application of data science including CLV is a not just a data and tools problem; it is a human problem. I interviewed **Jose Murillo**, chief analytics officer at Banorte Bank, the second largest financial group in Mexico, about how to secure budget for your data science projects. Under Jose's guidance, Banorte has yielded $1.8 billion since implementing CLV analysis, and recently leapfrogged Citibank and Santander Bank for market leadership in Mexico. Here is his advice.

How to Secure Budget for Customer-Centric Projects with Jose Murillo, Chief Analytics Officer at Banorte Bank

Can you tell us a little about your role as a chief analytics officer and how you discovered this topic?

Murillo: The analytics team, which I have led at Banorte since its inception, has been successful. We have yielded 1.8 billion dollars since CLV during our four-year tenure from a data science project. In tandem with the value that we have created, the size of the team increased. The reason that I'm drawn to this topic on how to gain the budget that you need to carry forward your projects, is because I think it's the foundational layer on which you can build a successful analytics data science practice.

That's interesting that you say that the ability to get budget is the foundational layer, not putting in certain technologies, or hiring people with an interesting mix of skills.

Murillo: Yes. The first piece that you must get is to have the budget. It's like Economics 101. If you recall your first course on economics, there are production possibilities. It determines how much output you can produce. The inputs depend largely on the budget that you're getting. Even more important for every person is their own productivity, which is the basis of their having a successful career. It hinges on how much capital, additional labor, and the technology they have access to. When I'm thinking about budget, that corresponds to how many people you can recruit in your team, the quality of the people that you're getting, and the technology that you have access to. That's largely the first determinant of how far you're getting the gain of analytics, data science, or for any project that you want to think about.

In many cases we assume, the organization either wants to do the program or they don't. I come up with a great idea. I bring my great idea to management. They should bless it and let me run with this idea. What's wrong with that picture?

Murillo: Yes, that's an excellent point. You would think that it should be self-evident, but it's not, and it happens that there are a lot of competing projects that require resources. And I think that's something we've found when we talked to our colleagues at conferences that they are really struggling to get the necessary budget. They are really smart people who are having a hard time securing the funds to have their ideas flourish, and that's not that uncommon. At the end of the day, within our industry people are a little bit shyer, and it is difficult for the C-suite to envision or the budget holder to envision what is the capacity of the data science you need that you are fielding. Also, data science units or analytics units are built largely as costs centers instead of profit centers. And in some sense, it is not expected for the data science to put some skin in the game to advance our projects. It's something that is expected to be largely subsidized by the corporation, which is non-sustainable in the long term.

What does it mean to be a profit center instead of a cost center? How does that change the internal thinking?

Murillo: The way that it changes is that you are going to grant budget, but you are expecting that the budget recipient is going to produce x times the budget that he's receiving. The way that most of the businesses are operated and the way it changes is that you are expecting that these data science units contribute to the bottom line, that it has a measurable ROI, and that it's accountable for yielding those results.

At the end of the day, you have most of the people that are going to grant the budget are not necessarily well versed on the technologies or the experts that your unit wants to hire. Probably there are profiles of people or technologies that haven't been purchased before at the company. And suddenly you are going to ask to hire a guy who is an artificial intelligence expert who can build random forest models. It's difficult to understand how profitable it is going to be for the company if I buy this technology or if I hire this type of people within the company. So, it's very much within the responsibility of the budget seeker to be clear and explain the potential. And sometimes the budget seeker is not even aware of how much he can make. It can be difficult in that sense.

You've been successful at communicating this internally. Do you have some examples or ways that you were successful at trying to get across these early data science ideas?
Murillo: I can show some successes and some blunders also. Initially it came like a blessing in disguise. It was not something that I planned initially when we built our analytics team in the sense that we were going to be held accountable in yielding 10 times our cost after the first year of operation. That's what I mean by "skin in the game," and it's literal in the sense that it's your personal wealth that's at risk or your job security in the worst case. The company's going to put at risk, a certain number of resources. And typically, what it happens is that, if you are thought of as a cost center, it's something that is just thrown into the well without any expectation of what is going to be produced. But when you are built as a profit center, the thought is that money is going to yield a certain return, and you are going to be held accountable. And so, you are willing to put your neck on the line. So yeah, you should be sure that if you're asking for a certain number of resources that you are going to put them to good use.

So going back to the examples that you asked me, data science analytics was a novel concept within the company. Banorte is a large financial group. You have 27,000 employees, and it's not like everybody's waiting to say, "Well, now the analytics team is coming, and that's just what we've been waiting for." You have to see who are going to be the early adopters, who are going to be your champions, whom you have and can work with, the ones that you are going to face less headwinds from in transforming the business. In our case it was the credit card business unit, which is now the most profitable project that we conduct. And the first project that we undertook which brought us a lot of credibility, was a cost-abatement project. The first year it contributed to the credit card unit to increase their profits from the previous year by 25 percent. When you pick the project, you have to be very careful because you know, cost projects are not really that difficult. You don't have to build a CLV. It's something perfectly easy to measure and to prove. It's something that can be quickly executed. In some sense, they can be like the low-hanging fruit.

When you say a cost abatement project, are you really talking about optimization the way we might think about it and the digital space?
Murillo: Yes, it's a cost-optimization project. It still has a lot of challenges because there are different stakeholders within the organization that have measured cost the same way for a bunch of years and suddenly there's a new novel way of doing it. There's still a lot of convincing to do. You have the idea, and then you have to sell the project. But when it's done, you are not going to have many discussions if it's really worth what you were saying it's worth because it's in the bookkeeping records. You can prove that very cleanly. In contrast, when you move to income revenue-generating projects, and you are acquiring a customer, you have to estimate the value of how much is that customer worth, and how much it's contributing to the customer equity of the firm.

Let me tell you a blunder because the success might seem easy, but I think it's also very easy to mess it up. For example, lately I've kept the exponential contribution of data science largely by doing experimentation projects. But the first experiments that we've run, they took a lot of time to get them done, and probably I really didn't pick the right projects. In that sense, I'd like to stress the point that [you should] pick the projects where you face less headwind.

I think that you need to build your reputation first before you tackle more challenging issues. That will create a very good dynamic, and I guess the most difficult part is to get seed capital. After you get the seed capital, and then you start delivering an ROI, then budget increases are much easier to get, and it's much easier to have a say on budgets that are complementary to your own success like IT investments or human capital investment.

So even in a large corporation you need to bring an entrepreneurial mindset in order to secure data budget. You need to paint a bigger picture, a bigger purpose, and then not focus on what does AI do and the mechanics of machine learning but focus instead on finding a great way to please our customers. Or, you can ask, "What if we solve this process or this problem and get people thinking about the bigger picture?"
Murillo: Yes, that's right, and especially for people who want to advance their careers and to have larger impact within their organization.

Do you look for entrepreneurs on your team to help do this?
Murillo: Yeah, let me tell you a little bit more. I funded my way through college by selling houses, and I was pretty successful at it. So yes, after doing a Ph.D. I thought that I would never use that skill, but it turned out to be pretty handy.

Going back to the time that I used to sell houses, customers really like explaining what was the product that I was selling. It's similar when you are doing a data science project. You have to be able to explain in a clear fashion what you're aiming for in a language that your colleague can relate to and that they can understand. They don't really need to understand all the dynamics of internal methodological issues on the models that you're building, but it has to make sense to them, and it has to be something that they can believe in that's credible.

When you are looking for ways to get people to believe in a certain idea, is there another example where you were able to not just get the seed capital but get everybody's heart on board as well?

Murillo: It's something that we've done with almost all our projects. We identify all the stakeholders that are necessary early on to discussion, because if you forget one of those, instead of a supporter or an ally, it might end up being a detractor. We are careful on who are the different stakeholders that need to be in a discussion. For example, one of the very recent projects that we're working on is based on the results that we've gotten from our experimentation. These are studies that we've done in behavioral analytics and artificial intelligence on the communication with our customers. We are refining the way that we're communicating to our customers through different channels, different products. And as you can imagine for every product, there are a bunch of stakeholders from its product-segment channels, and customer experience marketing. The way that it has worked is that we are holding daily meetings and seeing one product at a time. Initially it took a lot of investment in understanding how we want to communicate to our customers, how we want to standardize, and how we were going to build this champion upon which later we would put challengers to perfect the communication. And initially, the meetings were a little bit longer, but later on everybody agrees on different things. Everybody helps. So that's an important thing: that everybody's involved and so everybody has ownership on the project. And now that we've been doing this for the past three weeks, it's become a very expedited process. We've reached different agreements, and everybody knows it's going to be even harder to reverse to our old communication ways.

The way that we started the discussion was we had some internal mockups on which we had a large meeting with a bunch of stakeholders. And we did that for about a week. But the fact was that people are not necessarily that comfortable or willing to lean in and risk an opinion when you are facing the Ph.D.s and an expert on behavioral economics, and an expert on such-and-such, and an expert on product. People might be shy, and they might have really good ideas.

And what I found is that having five people and asking them in a more confined group improves discussion. I've sought people from not only my division but from other divisions. They pitched up really great ideas on what was missing in that communication. People who had experience on the front line and could see what was really missing. And it really fostered a very good collaborative exercise. It was not something that happened spontaneously, but it became our practice in some sense.

You use the smaller meetings before the larger meetings to get that collaboration?
Murillo: Yes. Instead of a group of 15 people, a group of five people, and alternating the people that were attending them. These people have really great ideas, and we ask them, "Would you be willing to put this forward in the big meeting?" And they did. And certainly, we ended up with a much more robust product at the end.

Now that I'm listening to you, something that I'm also thinking of that we've done within the larger group to foster these people to express their ideas, is really keeping it positive. We are very agnostic on what's a good idea or not, and what you want is to bend the highest paid person opinion (HIPPO). We really don't like that, because at the end any idea can be a good idea. Even if the group thinks that it's something that we might test, well we don't know. What we will do is we'll build a champion, and then we can test with a challenger to see if your idea makes sense, and it leads to higher conversions.

Are there any other examples that you want to share?
Murillo: Let me tell you one thing where I didn't get the budget that I wanted, and it probably made sense to not get the budget. At some point, I thought that it would be useful to have some analytics seminars for my colleagues in different departments to be more well versed on analytics and data science and that probably that would help to accelerate the process. The people from HR, told me, "Well, we are not really sure that people are going to get really excited about this." And when I talked to the people, they said, "Well, we feel pretty comfortable with you doing the analytics. Why do we need to learn

this?" I mean, in some sense I should have scouted and asked the people within other departments if they were interested in such a thing instead of me planning it from my office.

Let's say that I want to get budget for my company, what should I do? Where should I start?
Murillo: I think there are five issues. The first one is, I'm sure that you will have a set of transformative ideas. Select the one that has the least headwind. Pick the idea that you'd be more likely to be successful that's not going to be that surprising for your colleagues or the different stakeholders that you need to push forward. So that'd be the first one: Pick the right project.

The second one is building a business case that is very solid with the data, that is credible, that is believable.

After you've done that, the third thing that you need is convince yourself that you're really willing to put your neck on the line for it. You're going to ask that your company spend money on that project, so you have to be willing to risk something personally, so you have to be really convinced yourself. You're the one that has to be convinced first.

The fourth step is to understand very well who the budget gatekeeper is, and just state your case. If you don't get heard the first time, get into a loop in there. You are probably not communicating correctly so hone your sales pitch and address it to the right person. The way that you communicate to a person that is well versed in analytics and data science is that you can be much more succinct. But the pitch probably needs to be adjusted for the audience that you are already talking to.

And I guess the last part is that you need to measure what you've done. You need to measure the ROI and be willing to be held accountable for it and for good or for worse. Hopefully for good.

At Banorte, it was not enough to have a team of experts ready to do advanced customer analytics with high-quality data. To get and maintain funding, the analytics team needed to be the catalyst for change. That meant safely providing a way for people to feel they could speak up and add their ideas while also creating a sense of ownership. Through the sense of ownership, the teams aligned to work for the good of the customer and financial impact flowed.

How Leaders Capture More Customer Knowledge

Not every company has a clear view of their customers online or offline. Like many companies with a high number of quick-service stores, Starbucks customers rarely went to the website prior to purchasing their morning coffee. As a result, Starbucks could see the product sales data from each location, but not much about the customer. Although Starbucks launched a loyalty program in 2008, it seemed most customers were not overly compelled to use it. In 2009, Starbucks added the convenience of mobile payment through a bar code scan and usage eventually increased to 11 percent of retail sales volume as 2013 was winding down. Starbucks was already passing through the Learning Zone and in 2015, they upped their game to allow mobile payers to skip the line and also see new Starbucks products ahead of time. Mobile payments reduced friction, added convenience, and increased sales, but what Starbucks also created—whether accidentally or on purpose—was an ingenious way to capture all the customer knowledge which was previously stored in the local barista's brain.

If you were a regular at Starbucks, then your barista probably knew how you liked your coffee and may have even greeted you with something specific such as, "Will it be a tall Americano today, Ms. Hartsoe?" As convenient as that interaction might be, the way Ms. Hartsoe likes her coffee, and the timing of her orders was generally missing from the data. By pulling transactional data retroactively, Starbucks could have found interesting purchase patterns, but the ability to capture Ms. Hartsoe's attention in the moment was lost. So, Starbucks raised their game.

Starbucks literally gamified the mobile loyalty program with stars based on purchases, not visits, and a host of activities designed to both increase the cadence of purchases and expand the breadth of products purchased. Mobile app usage quickly rose with rave reviews and then when COVID hit, it exploded. Mobile orders now make up 25 percent of all Starbucks orders with a higher average ticket, increased customization and upsizing, and an all-time high food attachment. The active Starbucks Rewards member base with whom Starbucks directly communicates and provides personalized offers via the app increased in Q1 2020 to a record 21.8 million customers and a whopping 50 percent of company store sales. Now Starbucks has a tsunami of specific, personal, and authorized customer data pouring into fast databases. New customer analyses are guiding the company to deploy capital resources and drive innovation more effectively. In February 2021, Starbucks stock price hit $108, its highest ever since going public. Starbucks, like Nike, cites a growth mindset. But these stories are about much more than increasing customer transactions.

Both Starbucks and Nike have used their digital customer data to make personal, emotional connections with distinct customer groups while remaining financially strong. This only happens when there is a mutual agreeable exchange of value. The company seeks to serve the customer better and with more innovation, and the customer agrees this is valuable. This bonded connection is true loyalty, and through customer equity, it creates a measurable, long-term competitive advantage.

Innovation and Imitation

As Leaders emerge with new customer insights, the competition is quick to copy their innovations. Gillette's rivalry with Dollar Shave Club is a great example. In 2010, the hundred-year-old brand Gillette owned 70 percent of the razor market. Dollar Shave Club was founded in 2011, and by 2016 they had knocked Gillette's market share down to 54 percent. Dollar Shave Club's subscription service for men's grooming products (notably razors) was affordable, simple, and convenient. But moreover, the direct-to-consumer brand spoke to the heart of the customer in a modern voice that Gillette could not replicate. By 2017, Gillette launched their own copycat subscription service which was just getting going when early in 2019 Gillette released a disastrous ad. The ad featured pictures of what is considered "toxic masculinity" including bullying and sexual harassment but then encouraged men to challenge themselves to "do more that we can get closer to our best." Men did not appreciate the stereotype and defected to Dollar Shave Club in droves.

Michael Schrage, author of *Who Do You Want Your Customer to Become?* (Harvard Business Review, 2012) wrote at the time, "Customer lifetime value metrics should measure how effectively *innovation investment* increases customer health and wealth. Successful innovations make customers more valuable. That's as true for Amazon, Alibaba, Apple ... and Netflix. No one would dare argue that these innovators don't understand, appreciate, or practice a CLV sensibility." Gillette tried to originally meet the need of the customer with "shavetech" innovations and eventually a subscription service, but Dollar Shave Club not only delighted the customer, but they also aligned their innovation with the way the customer already saw themselves—money wise, handsome, and definitely not a sucker. As Schrage says, "making customers better, makes better customers."

Algorithms vs. Ethics

Can a company be too good at customer-centric transformation? Actually, yes. When the customer insights and data are flowing, a company must make an ethical choice about how to apply them. I often think algorithmic improvements follow a u-shaped curve where some improvement is good, but too much can be catastrophic.

Big Fish Casino is a story of customer-centric targeting gone wrong. A woman in Dallas who has no previous history with casinos online or offline, downloads a gaming app after hearing the tag line, "Play for free, play for fun." She starts to play with the free chips given by the app but when those run out, in-app purchases take over. At the end of the month, she's spent $8,000 in chips which she knows she cannot turn back into cash. She hides this from her husband and continues to play. Nine months later, the amount is now $40,000 and she knows she has a gambling addiction. She emails the Big Fish Casino customer service reps to cancel her account, block it, and ban her from the site. She requests this from them nearly a dozen times, but the company never closes and never blocks her account. Instead, they double down on her. They assign her a personal VIP rep who gives her free chips to keep her from leaving. He checks in with her daily.

He forms a friendship, and he finds out what's going on in her life. So much so that when Kelly's mother passes away, he actually sends flowers and ... more casino chips. In the end, she spends over $400,000.

Now a real casino would be required to cut her off or face fines, but online casinos have different regulations. In a presentation PBS unearthed by the developer of the casino's VIP strategy, we learn that 3 percent of the customers will return 90 percent of the value to the company. Now that is a lot lower than most companies that we look at where the high-value customer base is more like 17 percent, but the purchases are spread out a bit more. So, PBS then gets hold of some documents leaked from the actual program. If you look closely at the data, you'll see that they're tracking by individuals using the Facebook ID. They have age, sex, and a graph of that person's spend over time showing that a *whale*, a casino term for a high-value customer, is quickly ramping both in volume and frequency over an eight-month period. The casino quickly identifies a high-value customer, they hit them with a lot of marketing, and a VIP inside salesperson, and they refuse to stop.

Perhaps you're thinking that your company is not like a casino. But ask this: How you will know when your marketing, promotions, and your constant drive for sales are no longer building a healthy customer base? To be customer-centric is to listen, learn, and eventually lead customers by serving *their* best interests. Let me say that again: A customer-centric company exists to be of service to their customers, not to push product.

Tactics That Transform and Maintain Leadership

As companies enter the Leadership Zone, they understand the value of customer equity and how it relates to their business, but they face challenges operationalizing it. These tactics can help.

Technology that Transforms Leaders

When companies enter the Leadership Zone, they know customer data (and data overall) is a huge asset. Security becomes a stronger concern balanced with the business' need to be agile and responsive. There is a realization that the customer is the driver of business value and to see the customer, the data must be interlocked across everything the customer touches. That means your CRM, support, supply chain, marketing interlocks, optimizing customer relationships, and your view of them around all of these different datasets. If your product is digital, then that belongs in the mix as well. And at this point, they are able to stand up a rapid customer data analysis platform. This also means that machine learning starts to step into the process to solve for more automation, particularly as tested hypotheses are proven and move to personalization. Technology supports the flywheel of continuous customer-centric optimization.

Actions People Take as Leaders

Now the company is seeing a few larger-scale wins pay off. What was previously high risk is starting to be perceived as low risk due to all that supporting data. And that means that cross-business unit teams can start to emerge around optimization for CLV. Some customer-centric data is available in a self-service model, but more elaborate questions may need to be pulled by an analysis team with special skills to query the data. That leads to the question of accessibility for members who are not on that team. What some organizations do is require a test. If you pass, then you qualify for more direct access to large pools of data. This approach can help reduce the whole data democratization zoo which can happen if you give everybody training and full range access.

Early Leaders are having more discussion about their findings and that means knowledge sharing systems which hold definitions, previous findings, and other information start to become critical. This is an important socialization tool to keep surfacing good customer-centric insights and feed the formation of new hypotheses from across the company.

Leadership in the Leaders Zone

As companies enter the Leadership Zone, leadership is still centralized around the chief analytics officer (or similar C-level role) and their guidance includes aligning CLV applications to customer equity goals.[5] Centralizing financial definitions and formulas are a big part of this stage which in one approach or another eventually has to be blessed by the CFO. That basically means that if you're going to claim a win, that your project had $X of impact, then you'll need a financial person bless that and say "Yep. That's indeed the impact that we saw, our numbers agree, and we aligned."

Progression through this zone sees each member of the executive team agree to run by a small set of specific customer-centric metrics that interlock with company strategy and align to customer-centric tactics. The company takes the time to think about what those right metrics are, whether and how they can be measured, and what that means at all the layers of the organization. That's a big ask that will also create some discomfort as the organization changes focus.

At the end of the Leadership Zone, we have full company alignment. It is essentially the new normal and the critical achievement has become that the company is organized around the customer. The company is sensitive to customer changes as they happen such as new customers preferences, market changes, or even political changes. Internally you have everyone rowing in the same direction. So, you have a lot of internal collaboration up and down the chain for the good of the customer.

Processes that Support Leaders

As companies enter the Leadership Zone, the process to convert proven hypotheses from experiments into sensitive, contextual personalization and ultimately algorithms form a fast flywheel of learning. Running at a slower pace around this process is the larger systemic process of product changes to enable innovation. Company-specific, customer-centric algorithms and automation support and maintain the competitive advantage. It's not just the presence of CLV or customer data, but what the company does with it that creates the advantage.

But as companies move through this zone, they will soon see a need for ethics to cross-check the use of data. This cannot be automated because ethics is an inherently human judgment call related to current culture

• • •

5 It is interesting to see how organizations move this position around. It's very much in flux. There's no stable definition of where the CAO or CDO should go yet. It may even be a temporary role to support transformation until the company arrives at a new normal.

and the overall optics of a situation. Having human cross-checks on the automated outputs of machine learning and AI is important not only to understand how the answers were derived, but to provide a common-sense check that is impossible to program. As much as we call AI "artificial intelligence" it does not—and cannot—actually think. In order to protect ourselves from negative outcomes such as preying on the vulnerable, building up artificial demand bubbles, or deepening discrimination, we must have a human initially validate and then monitor results produced by AI. Laws are coming which will soon hold companies accountable for these algorithmic impact assessments.

Metrics for the Leadership Zone

For Leaders, we add ethical cross-checks and model security to prevent companies from sliding back down the curve. These are defensive measures that protect your progress. We also augment existing data with new external sources and seek executive alignment on customer value to help expedite your progress. These are offensive measures that accelerate progress. See Figure 5-1.

FIGURE 5-1

What to Measure in Leadership Zone

Measures That Protect	Measures That Accelerate
Listening Zone Still Applies	Custom Data Augmentation
Learning Zone Still Applies	Executive Alignment on Customer
Ethical Cross Checks	• Customer satisfaction
Model Security	• Predictors of customer value

Does everyone in every department understand and are they individually accountable for the same set of company-wide metrics that are continuously measured and specifically ladder from tactic to customer equity or a similar goal? The metrics of the company will change as a company gets hold of customer data and begins learning from it as the customer-centric insights start to flow.

At EA, a series of four player core metrics emerged which reflected critical new KPIs: scale, time, money, and loyalty. The metrics selected were trendable (meaning they can be tracked over time) and flexible (meaning they could easily be cut by brand or geography). Scale was the count of unique players. Some companies might use active customers. Time was the amount of time spent in the game. Some companies might use engagement online with their products. Money reflected average spending trends per customer. If the customer base is getting healthier, then the customer equity number (total CLV) will reflect this. And finally, loyalty was measured by Net Promoter Score (NPS). NPS measures the number of people who score how likely they are to recommend your product as a 9 or 10 ("promoters") minus the number who are less likely to recommend it by scoring it 6 or lower ("detractors"), ignoring the ones in the middle ("passives") who score it 6 or 7. Some companies might look at retention by customer cohorts instead, or even use both.

With metrics that flow across business units and up and down the corporate ladder, it becomes a bit more obvious how each tactical action helps or hinders the key metrics. That does not mean everything is known about the customer and how they affect the business. It does means that more people are able to drive by the company-wide metrics that are set, and these metrics are measured and aligned in a very logical way across the board.

Exit Criteria

Once companies become Leaders, the only criteria is to not lose ground to competitors. Ask these key questions:

- Does the CEO believe customer data is a competitive advantage?
- Is the company fully aligned and organized to dynamically serve the customer?

If you were to ask someone how they contributed to the customer and to the equity that's generated from each customer, they would know, and they would have an answer. Now live, aligned intelligent customer-centric data is just part of doing your job.

Our goal at the end of a customer-centric transformation is to relate to people individually, personally, meaningfully at scale with the tools that we have so that we can create more happy customers, and simultaneously, healthier businesses. Ultimately the corporations should be of service to the customer.

How Poshmark Leads a Customer-Centric Culture with Barkha Saxena, CDO of Poshmark

Barkha Saxena, chief data officer at Poshmark, joined me on my podcast to talk about scaling with data. Barkha shares how her team added the customer-centric layers to boost both the intelligence behind the data as well as the value for the community. This sense of a "data-driven heart" has fueled Poshmark's exponential growth from a start-up to IPO in 2021. Here is part of our conversation.

Tell us a little bit about how you got to be part of the Poshmark team and then also a little bit more about Poshmark.

Saxena: I joined Poshmark in March 2014. I had just quit my job, and I was trying to figure out what I was going to do next. I wanted to stay in the data field and was looking for something in either the mobile or ecommerce space, which is when I found Poshmark and decided to reach out to its founder and CEO, Manish Chandra, to start a conversation. Poshmark was only two years in with 35 or so people working at the company. As I met with more and more people, I fell in love with the team and I loved the concept of trying to build an online fashion marketplace that included a social aspect, which was very unique. I was very excited about the role data could play in there, and I got to do that with really fun people.

What is the culture like working at Poshmark? I've been thinking a lot about customer-centric cultures, and it strikes me that Poshmark probably has this.

Saxena: It's a very people-centric company and the best way to understand that is through our four core values: focus on people, lead with love, together we grow, and embrace your weirdness. We apply these four values internally when we work together, as well as with the community we are serving. We say "focus on people" because we are in the service of our community. With every decision we make, we think of our community and how it will help them. Similarly, internally, every decision starts with being people-focused, and then we lead with love, and that helps in so many decisions. Whenever in doubt, lead with love, and things will become much clearer. We say "together we grow" because we focus on each and everyone's individual growth. We also look at it from the community perspective because Poshmark is only going to grow if our community is growing with us, and they are benefiting from Poshmark's growth. And lastly, we embrace all weirdness. It is such a powerful thing because what we are saying is we embrace all diversity. Everyone with any convictions or title are welcome at Poshmark, whether it's an employee or one of our community members. The underlying theme of all four values is the people, and that makes Poshmark so much fun. It's a company where really smart people focus on working together in creating a product that is building a community and bringing people closer together. People who are passionate about fashion, but doing it in a very selfless way, where everyone focuses on the other person's goals, which allows the whole company to grow together.

If you think of it, we are not a huge company. In September 2019, we announced that our sellers had earned over $2 billion, and $1 billion of that happened in just the last year. This shows that we are able to achieve that despite still being a smaller company. We have over 500 people at the company, but we are all working together with a common goal of serving our community. It creates a beautiful culture, and for me, it feels like another home.

I can see why you love working there. Can you tell us a little bit more about your specific role and what your team does?
Saxena: At the highest level, my function exists to create value

for the community, but we look to create that value through data. My team works across all the business functions from growth, marketing, and product to operations, finance, and accounting. I look at all the data to see how we can use it to keep building the product which will bring the highest ROI to each of these functions and the community. To give you an example, my team is divided into multiple vertical teams, which are very closely aligned with each of the business functions. The head of my product data team works with the product and engineering teams and is focused on how we can use data to help the team build the best product, experience, and community. Similarly, when my head of growth and marketing team is working with his counterpart business partners, he's very focused on figuring out how we can use data to continue to retain our users, deliver a great experience, and bring new users on board who are benefiting from the uniqueness of Poshmark's social marketplace.

Do those different areas ever conflict where you have a product wanting to understand one thing from a particular angle versus a different part of the business?
Saxena: I have been in multiple places, so I completely understand where that question is coming from. It does not happen at Poshmark, and I think there are multiple reasons I have not seen that happen. No function exists for the sake of its own function. We all exist in the service of our community. People can have different ideas for what will deliver us that value, but that's where I think data plays a beautiful role because data is very objective. You need to start questions with context and some ideas, but then when you take those questions and you start looking at them from the data perspective, you always find the answer, which is very objective, not driven by any biased opinion. My team is also an independent team— we are not part of the product team nor the growth and marketing team, so we look at it without bias, which is very important and something our business partners respect.

If a product manager is trying to build a feature and says, "Hey, I want to be able to recommend a good, personalized set of listings to my users," they don't try to influence how we are going to look for the answer to that question. They leave the question to us and let us figure it out. Because of Poshmark's culture, we all look at the picture holistically, and then data becomes a unifying denominator that comes up with a comprehensive story.

Manish is a very data-driven functional person. There aren't too many startups who hire a data leader at an early stage when it's only a 35-person company. Manish did that because he believed in the power of the data, and he has instilled this in our culture.

Manish and I both operate the same way in that we want the team to figure it out. The reason we have really smart people who are focused in that area is because they have the expertise and insights about the user behavior so they can do a much better job of connecting what the question is and then listing the hypothesis in partnership with their business partner. They say, "Here are some of my thoughts. What do you think are the additional things we should be looking at here?" One of the unique and valuable things we do at Poshmark is get the opinion of someone who is not from that business function to get a different perspective that we might have missed.

That sounds very efficient. It sounds very agile. Barkha, when you first started at Poshmark, did you have to wrestle with the data to get things to queue up so you could answer their questions or was it all greenfield and you could get ahead of it because you came in so early?
Saxena: Before working at Poshmark, I spent my time in bigger companies and my job was to just start working with the data. Poshmark was the first startup I worked at, and what I learned on my first day was that we didn't have too much data, so my first three years at Poshmark were spent in building the whole data infrastructure. That was a blessing because as I built the data infrastructure, I built it with the end goal in mind that when I'm done with this process, what I wanted to see was how this data will be enabling decisions across all business functions and what tools I would need. I started with a high-level vision and then mapped it down to the multi-year execution steps.

Because we started with how this data will deliver value to the business, we were very intentional in deciding how we were collecting data, and what data culture we were setting up. Not everyone has the benefit of starting fresh, but I did, which was great. It was me and one data engineer from our team in India. We spent time defining the metrics, specifically the top 30 priority metrics we should focus on.

Trends can be interpreted in two different ways, so I created like a structure that showed how we should be looking at the dimensions. The definitions are consistent so that when we get together, we are no longer discussing what the data is; we're discussing the trends, what it means, and how we make our decisions.

I've heard across other companies that the metrics that you pick and your framework for evaluation need to be trendable and extensible through the organization. I was a little bit surprised to hear you say the top 30 metrics, because I've heard other companies go down to more like three or four, and then they unpack them from that base of three or four. But you mentioned 30. Is that still the case?

Saxena: It's actually many more than that now, but we have a process on how we keep track of it. We are in the social commerce space, which means we have many more metrics we need to track as compared to the typical ecommerce company. These 30 metrics are across all the business functions—there are metrics the growth team needs to track to see how different channels are performing, there are metrics the product team needs to track to understand how users are engaging, and then there are metrics our community team tracks to make sure they are serving our customers in the best way. As a data team owner, it is my responsibility to keep track of those 30 metrics and come up with the key insights to share with the whole executive team.

We have clear data literacy at Poshmark because we educated every executive and their teams on what the metrics mean and how they should be looked at. There are different business owners for various metrics, but my team brings it all together and communicates it to the team because if you leave any of the functions in silos, you will miss the full picture.

Are you using customer lifetime value or some of the components of customer lifetime value?
Saxena: We absolutely do. To give you an example of that, if we were making decisions just based on what a user does on the first day of the first week, we would be making so many not-great decisions or at least not high-ROI decisions. Our user cohort goes through the smiley curve as we call it internally, which means like any other ecommerce company or any social company, you'll get a lot of users on board, and then the cohort has stabilized at some point. It's a very standard cohort curve. What happens with Poshmark is there is an initial decay where some of the users don't have the same high value as they did on day one. But once they get to the stable point and then start to grow, that's what we call the Poshmark love effect, or you can call it the social network effect.

If we were not looking at it from the customer lifetime value, we would have a very different picture of different cohorts and channels and how they lead to it because the picture is not complete.

But it's not just a great experience.
Saxena: We use data to make sure the experience is very personalized. We present you an experience based on the way you are using the app, whether it's who we recommend you should connect with, recommending the items you should purchase, or thinking about what seller tools we should be building. We need to think about different segments of buyers and sellers as opposed to just looking at them as one lens.

You've really taken heterogeneity through data into an exponential level and found not just ways to collect it but ways to collect it meaningfully so that you know what behaviors are actually driving a difference for your business. And I think right there is where you quantified what you call the love effect, and you can see people so happy to have a new tool that matters to them or the ability to share it with their friends or whatever personalization or recommendation that you're layering in. Are there any other examples that you want to share before we talk about how somebody should think about their data structures?

Saxena: When we built our A/B testing platform, we wanted to build it in such a way that we could get insights into multiple phases. Really early on, the data matures and then we are really confident, so we wanted to be able to do this in a very automated way. As a startup, we needed to be very efficient, but we still needed to have the statistics of measure make sense.

We looked at a lot of external A/B testing tool options, but we decided to build an internal A/B testing tool because there's a lot of things that are unique to Poshmark from the data customer perspective. Comparing 2020 to 2019, we were able to output 75 percent more A/B testing analysis because we brought efficiency into the process and because we educated our entire product engineering team so that as they start to send out insights, there is no confusion.

I think that's the problem when you start putting in all these different tools and trying to cobble together a stack from external tools. People don't really understand how things are collected or built. Your ability to have more fun with the data is directly related to the way you've built the stack.

Saxena: Absolutely. And that's why we have made very heartful decisions on what tools we select and how it will fit into the Poshmark ecosystem.

In January 2020, I wrote an article about measuring the ROI of the data team. In that article, I shared that the purpose of a two-dimensional metrics table is that one side shows the different business functions, and the other side shows how data adds value to the business. For example, there is so much excitement around AI and machine learning that a lot of times people don't realize 70-80 percent of the value gets delivered without that.

A lot of the schools are selling machine learning in such a way that everyone thinks that's all the mathematicians do when in reality, that's what we do for the problems where that makes sense. Even then, you need to bring in the business judgment and the human intelligence. For example, if we would have built Poshmark's recommendation with the goal of "Let's build the best recommendation algorithm from the data we have," it would be a different answer than, "Let's build an algorithm which will delight user experience at Poshmark." Why? Because people come to Poshmark to find a variety of products, so we've built something very different, with human elements added to it.

It's like driving a car, looking out the rearview window.
Saxena: Exactly.

At Poshmark, data is accessible to managers across the business, but they are not solely responsible for understanding all the insights. It is a strategic partnership. Moreover, Poshmark's data team has a specific purpose: To increase ROI, drive strategic growth initiatives, uncover and drive new opportunities, and drive scaling initiatives or build new capabilities. Companies cannot become successful customer-centric leaders without the data team positioned as a strategic partner within the organization.

● ● ●

CUSTOMER-CENTRIC TAKEAWAYS

→ Leaders consistently fight to hold their place against internal forces such as budget pressures and external forces such as imitators.

→ To maintain Leadership, these companies need to align well internally, and execute quickly. Sometimes this means using their own tools that are shaped to their unique business needs.

→ Customer-centric leaders pause when releasing algorithms or when making complicated decisions to carefully consider the customer benefit and response.

➜ Customer-centric leaders are not just selling more; they generate an emotional resonance with their customer that compels these customers to re-engage again and again. This appears as increasing or compounding customer equity quarter over quarter (or year over year).

CHAPTER 6

What We Could Ultimately Gain

EARLY IN the 2000s, I recall having a very pointed conversation with a friend of mine. I was running a high-flying, venture-backed company and she was (and still is) a class action attorney in San Francisco. I said that companies had an incredible opportunity to do good, and given less government regulation, they had the power and resources to become part of the social fabric in a mutually beneficial way. She said that companies were always misbehaving because they would always do what benefited the bottom line and, as a result, they often had to be sued or regulated to be kept in line. Does a company exist to deliver shareholder value, typically measured as profit, first?

On August 19, 2019, the Business Roundtable, a group of powerful CEOs who meet to consider public policy, said no. The Business Roundtable currently includes about 200 companies such as 3M, Abbott, BlackRock, Bristol Myers Squibb, Boeing, The Home Depot, IBM, Johnson & Johnson, Lockheed Martin, Marriott, Macy's and more. The statement said:

Americans deserve an economy that allows each person to succeed through hard work and creativity and to lead a life of meaning and dignity. We believe the free-market system is the best means for generating good jobs, a strong and sustainable economy, innovation, healthy environment, and economic opportunity for all.

While each of our individual companies serves its own corporate purpose, we share a fundamental commitment to all of our stake holders. We commit to:

- *Delivering value to our customers. We will further the tradition of American companies leading the way in meeting or exceeding customer expectations.*
- *Investing in our employees. This starts with compensating them fairly and providing important benefits. It also includes supporting them through training and education that helps develop new skills for a rapidly changing world. We foster diversity and inclusion, dignity, and respect.*
- *Dealing fairly and ethically with our suppliers. We are dedicated to serving as good partners to the other companies, large and small, that help us meet our missions.*
- *Supporting the communities in which we work. We respect the people in our communities and protect the environment by embracing sustainable practices across our businesses.*
- *Generating long-term value for shareholders, who provide the capital that allows companies to invest, grow, and innovate. We are committed to transparency and effective engagement with shareholders.*

Each of our stakeholders is essential. We commit to deliver value to all of them, for the future success of our companies, our communities, and our country.

They go on to say, "We commit to deliver value to all of them for the future success of our companies, our communities and our country." And that's the end of the statement.

I think it is very revealing that shareholder value was moved to point number five. Customer value is point number one, employee value number two, suppliers are number three, community is number four and number five is, of course, shareholder value. The commitment to deliver value to all is present, but it does not say equally. The order that they're listed is actually quite relevant. Also note the emphasis on long-term value for shareholders, which is a subtle (or maybe not-so-subtle) pushback on the short-term, quarterly pressure from Wall Street.

The statement was generally well-received, except by the organizers of the B Corporation movement. B Corporations are a relatively new type of business which is legally required to balance profit and purpose. They typically meet extremely high standards for social and environmental goals as well as corporate transparency and accountability. The B Corporation movement responded by pointing out to the Business Roundtable they have been doing this all along, and their version is legally binding in a majority of states. They took out a full-page ad in the Sunday *New York Times*. It said in big bold letters: **Let's get to work.**

Then the ad continued:

> *Dear Business Roundtable CEOs, we are part of a community of certified B Corporations who walk the walk of stakeholder capitalism. We are successful businesses that meet the highest standards of verified, positive impact for our workers, customers, suppliers, community, and the environment. We operate with a better model of corporate governance, benefit corporate governance, which gives us and could give you a way to combat short-termism and the freedom to make decisions to balance profit and purpose.*
>
> *As you know, with continued resistance from investors on this new definition of business, we've got work to do to help them see that stakeholder governance builds trust and builds value. More importantly, it also ensures that the purpose of capitalism is to work for everyone and for the long-term, let's work together to make real change happen.*

That's pretty sharp and it's signed by Patagonia, Allbirds, data.world, Ben and Jerry's, Stash Tea, Stumptown Coffee Roasters, and others. In addition to being B Corps, what do all those companies have in common? Velocity. They use data, including customer data, to really know their customers, then be of service to their customers. And that in turn generates loyalty, which in turn ignites a virtuous cycle of customers coming back again and again. I personally believe that one year of customer-centric business thinking is worth about three years of traditional product-centric thinking. Why? Because we are in a new customer-centric age and customers are empowered and voting with their wallets. It is every company's job now to listen to them, learn from them, and lead innovations that truly do make the world a better place. The time is now.

CUSTOMER EQUITY ACCELERATOR INTERVIEW

The New Board Metrics: Environmental Social and Governance (ESG) with Jim Deiotte, Executive Director of the Master of Professional Accountancy Program at the University of California

Jim Deiotte, Executive Director of the Master of Professional Accountancy Program at the University of California joined me on the podcast to talk metrics. The program Jim oversees is anchored in emerging data use technologies as well as the practical, legal, and ethical uses and application of data. In our conversation, we explored the future of business metrics that report on ESG (environment, social, and governance) and how customers are demanding more accountability from the companies they buy from. Here are some highlights from our conversation.

> *Could we start by briefly recapping how company value is traditionally measured?*
> **Deiotte:** Basically, we measure the success of a company by looking at what we did yesterday. How do we perform? How do we utilize our assets and our talents and our people? How do we develop new products? And it worked for close to 200 years, but we have a new dynamic taking place today.

BlackRock and their CEO, Larry Fink, said that BlackRock is becoming a lot more customer-centric by putting all their weight behind sustainability and climate change because their investors are demanding it. Most people talk about this as ESG reporting. Can you tell us a little bit more about what ESG reporting is and why this move from BlackRock was so significant?

Deiotte: Larry Fink issued a letter to his investor community in January, but this was just one of the items that are really adding on to a tipping point of a considerable change on how boards are going to hold themselves accountable to not only their shareholders but also other stakeholders of that organization. Larry Fink basically threw in his organization, and they manage roughly $7 trillion in investment assets and things. Listen, if a company is not really thinking about the ESG, environment, social and governance of the organization and reporting it continuously, we're not going to look at them as much.

We're going to basically begin to differentially invest in other places to take. And so, there's an immediate reaction out there in the community asking, how do I hold myself accountable?

One of the things I'll share with you that I think is exciting is what the four largest accounting firms in the world have put together. It was a paper that basically begins to attach metrics to this so they can compare the organizations. And that's the importance of that reporting of what's taking place.

You talk about ESG as environment, social, and government, but the word I'm missing there is customer. Where does the customer fit in that ESG framework?

Deiotte: It's embedded in the social side. It's the relationships an organization has with its key stakeholders. This is about how the boards becoming responsible to management that has to articulate clearly where they're going, how they're creating value. And this is a much more complex conversation because it's not only where are we growing value, but also to whom are we growing this value for? The one we're most comfortable with is the people who make the financial funds available to the company as a shareholder. That's not changing except for the perspective, but now we're adding in how you're supporting government and regulators. Are you engaged with them? Do you know where they're trying to take and improve society? Tell us where you are in your communities, where you're doing business. What are you doing for your employees? And last, and I don't mean by any stretch least, what are you doing for your customers? How often do we go out and absolutely articulate the level of investment I'm making in my customers, and most importantly is my customer acknowledging they know this investment was made in them?

The way the internet is these days [customers] can really affect the way business is being done, and commerce is happening with organizations. In the past, the response to unhappy stakeholders has been much more reactive. They've picketed. They boycotted; they've gotten in front of shareholders. It's been more of a squeaky wheel. Now, when I look at the customer stakeholder, they have the most interesting way of boycotting. They just simply don't buy products. The customers just quietly disappear. Engagement with the customer is one of the most important things that we can do in our business. The shift is really not to react, but to be proactive.

Could you talk a little bit about some of the metrics that are getting developed to help corporations see where they're healthy and where they're not?

Deiotte: There's a number of things that we're seeing emerge as a standard out there in the industry. It's customer interactions. How often are you connected? Would they refer you to somebody else that would be interested in buying your product? There are ones that show that you can get a temperature of a customer in terms of what they're likely to do in terms of supporting your product.

How do you understand some of the pains they have that are not related to, for example, the product they're purchasing? Do you supply a product that is in alignment with their needs? I think what's going to happen is the conversations really have to become much more expansive in the way we understand what our customers need, not just for today, not just for tomorrow, but what they're seeing as their long-term challenges, really aligning with that.

The second thing is, if I get asked a question by a board member, who says, "Show me how we're investing in our customers. Show me how you're really determining this, that this return on investment is being accepted by the customer," they acknowledge it. They appreciate it. And if all you do is walk in there with simply a corporate survey that's been done with your customers, that is a data point. But I think what people are looking for are more independent ways of making certain that that information isn't biased, that we ask the right customers—not just the ones that wanted to respond. If you can, get more independent data points that really give you an idea of where that customer is going or where they should be going and how you can influence and support them in their long-term efforts. I think you have a much more powerful relationship. And I think it's one that's going to satisfy boards in the future.

A lot of people use Net Promoter Score or other very soft metrics. What you're talking about is more independent ways to value the customer voice, or perhaps to value the corporation. Can you talk more about some of these test metrics that companies are trying out in order to measure their business in a future-forward fashion?

Deiotte: The customers are one of our core stakeholders. The more I understand, the more I can get into the understanding of the challenges that customer's dealing with, the better off I am in terms of being able to meet their needs. Maybe that's sitting down with customers and saying, "This product that we've been selling for a long time or the service that we've been providing, we really need to help you take it another direction." And that form of engagement is much more intimate. It's a much more trusted relationship that you're getting, but it's something that really gives you more of a direction and where you're actually trying to partner with that customer on how both of you can advance successfully in the future.

I think it's a different type of conversation that's going to take place where everybody's looking at that value chain that they're part of looking back at them and saying, "Where am I getting my stuff?" And more importantly, "Where's my stuff going?" I don't think that form of information is readily out there. I think this is a different type of question being asked because we have never really gone in and articulated in a public way. How are you investing in that customer? If I value our great customer relationship, I may show it by delivering my product faster, giving you a better price, giving you a better volume, getting my best people. There's a lot of things that I can deliver.

So that sounds like a metric about stakeholder engagement, where the organization's approach to stakeholder engagement might be around the frequency of engagement by the type of stakeholder group and their processes of how they ensure the reliability of that information. So that could be one of our metrics: stakeholder engagement.

Deiotte: I'm going to give you a really good example about digital transformation. In today's Wall Street Journal, there's an announcement of another group that's buying RadioShack, again. RadioShack doesn't exist. You can't go to RadioShacks. They're being bought because it's a 100-year-old enterprise that has an eplatform that still has value in it. And people are still trying to figure out how to manage these relationships and how to gain greater insights on it. You will see a number of bankrupt companies that are going to happen this year, and people are going to be buying the data. They're going to be looking for the information they're trying to get a pulse on. What was the IQ of that organization? Is it entirely gone? And how can I maybe grab some of that information and, again, grow my own insights out there? So, this area is one of those that if you are doing business with customers that really can answer, or if they can't even answer what the definition of digital transformation is, you really need to have a one-on-one with them and say, "Listen, we really like you. You're our customer, after all. Can we help you out? Can we sit down and have a conversation with you? We really want to help you because we're dependent upon you at the end of the day."

Are there metrics yet that businesses are testing out in order to try to bring in all of this ESG goodness?
Deiotte: You barely have the conversation taking place, let alone what I'd call the development of those metrics that you could sit down and say, "Hey, are we actually making this investment? And do we do a good job?" One of the darlings of ESG, was Pacific Gas and Electric, but it's now in bankruptcy. Just because you are ESG and you are reporting that way doesn't necessarily mean you're going to be successful. But more importantly, is people are now asking the question, "How did that company get into the ESG fund?" You know, what metrics were they sharing with us that would suggest they really are ESG aligned, friendly, and supportive? Now, I'm not suggesting that this company shouldn't have been in that fund. What I'm suggesting is that people are having difficulties of splitting between asking, "Is this a marketing thing that's going on? Or is this truly a company that's embracing this concept of stakeholder engagement and looking at different ways of creating value, both for the financial owners and other stakeholders within that organization?"

What metrics should a company be thinking about or even testing now to help respond to the different stakeholders of which customer is part of that?
Deiotte: Actually, if you put a mirror to the situation, if you're not asking that of your customers, it means you're not asking that question of your suppliers as well. And that's a weakness within your organization. It really is taking a look at what are you valuing in terms of the relationships that you're procuring your goods and your services from. One of the ones that's out there, and it is out there in a pretty consistent way, is Net Promoter Score. These are independently verified. Would you recommend so-and-so to your product, your service, what you're trying to do? And that's a really good one. It's one that you should be using in terms of evaluating

your own performance. But it's also important in terms of the way you're looking at the people of the organizations you're buying your product from.

Social engineering or social span, what your involvement is, is another one where people are going to be asking you, "Can you tell us about the stakeholders in the communities that you're supporting? Let us see the involvement of your executives and your people. Are they on boards? Are they involved in the community? How much time is committed to the community to help out, maybe with local school matters or environmental matters within your community?" There's a scoring that will be created around those lines. I think it's identifying clearly that you're a supporter of us, and we want to make sure that we understand your concerns and cares. And again, it's within your employees, it's in within government, it's within your supply chain. And again, with your customers, the most important one, you have to be engaged and there has to be a quality of engagement. The more you can get it supported by third parties getting involved and providing that independent thought and confirmation, that's just simply going to be more powerful.

The last one is your R&D. If you're not looking at the people you're supplying and they're not doing any research and development or development of their products and services better, your strength is going to be earned by their weakness. And so, it goes the same way. Companies are looking at these and saying, "Tell us about how you're investing in your people. How are you getting them ready for digital transformation? How are you using our information better? Are you protecting the private information that we're giving you, and how do you do so, give me comfort around that?" I think these are some of the measurements that you're going to start seeing more and more frequently. And as people become more familiar with it as a test, it's going to get better and better over time. I know who my stakeholders are. Let those stakeholders know. Let them also know that you're making an investment in them begin that process of mutual engagement on how to best serve each other, and then document it and look for ways of making improvements on it going forward.

And you know, I love when you talk about these measures over time. To me, that means that every metric that comes into the business reporting at the top is trendable and sliceable through the rest of the organization. The thing I would worry about is if I'm the CEO of a new company that's using this metrics approach; you can't always have everything go up into the right. And yet Wall Street absolutely hammers companies when they don't hit one of those metrics going up into the right. How are companies dealing with this vulnerability?

Deiotte: When I look at integrated reporting that's taken place, they are required, not just your financial statement results of what yesterday was, not just an opinion on the controls you have in your organization for better decision-making. But can you articulate clearly and share with the world your business model? How do you create value? And people are nervous about that. So that's a problem. The second one is they have to sit down, and they have to share both in short term, medium term, and long term. These are some of the business decisions ahead of us, and that's scary, but I also have to go and articulate what are the consequences of inaction or action.

People are really saying you've got to be more transparent. If I have a business model that creates value, and I'm part of an ecosystem, it's building a stronger business, a stronger ecosystem for that industry, a stronger community. And you create, again, the bottom line of a more sustainable enterprise.

I've always felt that customer equity leads you to a more sustainable enterprise. But what I'm hearing behind what you say are the speed with which a company is comfortable with change is moving. And the innovation alongside that is also moving. By definition, companies can't be just doing the same thing every day. Otherwise, the competitors are going to catch up.

Deiotte: One of the areas that I enjoy keeping a strong tab on is mergers and acquisitions. One of the things that we try to squeeze out in a deal is basically fulfilling the synergies that we thought we were going to have entering an acquisition or combination. When I look at the area around the sales, where we expect, because of combination, we're going to grow more. We're going to have more profit where we're going to do all this. It sounds great in the press release. I'm not talking about just goodwill, I'm talking about the value of my customers that can be integrated, that I can transfer. I can share that these insights carry over. That's creating value for your enterprise for the long term. That's creating a saleable value for the future. And right now, executives aren't thinking that way.

They're not sitting back and thinking, "If I were to be an attractive suitor at some point in time, what would they see in terms of our customers?" I use the term "glob of goodwill," which to me is almost impossible to manage. I think the focus in this intensity on the customer focus is really going to become big. But I think it's really going to go up another gear to become more and more familiar to tell us what you're doing around this stakeholder and how you're creating value between the two of you.

And I think that becomes most obvious when you talk about RadioShack, where somebody bought that company for the data assets. These are now seen as valuable.
Deiotte: Allison, you've been in this business a really long period of time. And you understand the quality of information, the algorithms that produce an insight, that combination is complex to put together. It's a difficult task. If I can basically leverage into the experiences, the experiments, the efforts of successes and failures of a failed company, I can learn from some of the things that they did or didn't do. That's a value to me to understand what they're trying to do. Then the only difference, the only real question, is the allocation of value to you versus everybody else that's really serving the customers they're ultimately serving.

Let's take this down to the tactical level. Let's say that I'm convinced, and I want to help guide my management team to reflect the value we provide to different stakeholders. What should I do?
Deiotte: I think you have to simplify the challenge. Nobody has to do this, but we shouldn't get necessarily started right now. We're

getting ahead of the car. No, I think this is a change that's occurring. You need to really begin to educate yourself as to where it might possibly go because it's not the reporting. It's the cultural shift that takes place within the organization that matters. The second thing is, look at deals today. What's going on. Most of these transactions are being bought are considerable. Then the percentage of the acquisition that's going to fix assets like building and inventory and other assets is really pretty small. Eighty-five percent of it is going to be intangible. If that's being the case, look at the key intangibles that are there (a workforce in place, research and development and process) and let's put down their customers.

I look at the other stakeholders that are involved, but the stakeholder that matters to me most is my customer. They're the ones that are bringing money into my organization, in addition to the investors that are hoping to make money from that effort. I just don't think enough time has been spent with customers and understanding the value that they can confer. And with this flow of data that's happening out there right now, I think you can really solidify and prove out greater portions of value on your customer relationships.

Final Thoughts

The pressure is on for companies to provide more accountability to a broader set of stakeholders across environmental, social, and governance (ESG) reporting. Customers not only fit the social component but create a powerful measurement link. Customers today choose to purchase from companies that agree with their broader ESG values, and they expect this information to be transparent. The best way to respond to this pressure is with a customer-centric data strategy that aligns the health of your company with the benefit of the customer.

Whether your company is in the Listening, Learning, or Leadership Zone, there are specific actions you can take today that will help you become more quantifiably customer centric. For companies in the Listening Zone, the name of the game is to first enable trusted data and kick off a cultural change via well-shaped reporting. When a company reaches the Learning Zone, a major transition occurs enabled by the combination of growing experimentation, CLV-focused measures, and fast-flowing data lakes. Ultimately, arrival in the Leadership Zone codifies experiments into algorithms, and aligns the organization around the customer so innovation can take hold.

Throughout this book I've emphasized customer lifetime value as a key component of a customer-centric strategy. If there is anything we learn from leaders, it is the heartfelt emotional bond that customers share with these brands. CLV allows us to align our teams and balance financial performance with that sensitive bond, and ultimately provides ample opportunities to "lead with love" as Poshmark's Barkha Saxena says.

If ever there was a metric to measure the "goodness" of a company, then customer equity is it. The techniques I've laid out in this book are data-driven strategies to expedite your company's transformation to sustainable customer-centric leader. Imagine if every company were such a sensitive leader seeking to deeply serve customers' needs rather than simply sell more product at lower cost. Could the world be a better place? This is the promise of customer equity. Starting today, you too can use these powerful tools to do good. Let's get there together.

• • •

CUSTOMER-CENTRIC TAKEAWAYS

- ➜ It is abundantly clear that increasing shareholder value is no longer a sufficient basis on which to run a company.

- ➜ Customer equity can be seen as an ESG calculation at the board level, and part of the new metrics shaping company's social responsibilities.

- ➜ By using the proper techniques outlined in this book, companies can find the sweet spot of mutual benefit where company value increases lockstep with the value delivered to happy customers. Healthy companies have happy customers.

APPENDIX

Supplemental materials may be found at the author's website, **www.ahartsoe.com**, including a maturity curve quiz, videos, ebook, and the entire *Customer Equity Accelerator* podcast series.

For speaking engagements, bulk book orders, or media requests, including having Allison as a guest on your podcast visit **www.ahartsoe.com.**

Finally, if your company has questions and would like hands-on strategic support for your journey toward customer-centric maturity contact us at **info@ahartsoe.com** or visit **www.ahartsoe.com/contact** to schedule a conversation.

RESOURCES

Ambition Data: eLearning Series
- ambitiondata.com/resilience

Ambition Data: Discounting Framework
- ambitiondata.com/should-companies-discount-during-covid

Ambition Data: Nine Questions to Ask Any Technology Vendor
- ambitiondata.com/wp-content/uploads/2020/07/Nine-Questions-for-Technology-One-Pager.pdf

Customer Equity Accelerator Podcast
- ambitiondata.com/podcast

Customer-Based Corporate Valuation Paper for Non-Contractual Firms
- papers.ssrn.com/sol3/papers.cfm?abstract_id=3040422

Customer-Based Corporate Valuation Paper for Contractual Firms
- papers.ssrn.com/sol3/papers.cfm?abstract_id=2701093

Customer Centricity: Focus on the Right Customers for Strategic Advantage
- amazon.com/Customer-Centricity-Customers-Strategic-Essentials/dp/1613630166

**Customer Centricity Playbook: Implement a Winning Strategy
Driven by Customer Lifetime Value**
- amazon.com/Customer-Centricity-Playbook-Implement-Strategy/
  dp/1613630905/

**Measuring the Digital World: Using Digital Analytics
to Drive Better Digital Experiences**
- amazon.com/Measuring-Digital-World-Analytics-Experiences/
  dp/0134195086/

Who Do You Want Your Customers to Become?
- amazon.com/gp/product/B008HRM9X4/

The Truthful Art: Data, Charts and Maps for Communication
- amazon.com/Truthful-Art-Data-Charts-Communication/
  dp/0321934075/

ACKNOWLEDGMENTS

Someone once told me I had spent a lot of time gathering input, but the real question was, "What will you do with it, Allison?" I'd like to thank that person and all the others who helped me get off my backside and start using my voice to spread these powerful ideas.

This book would not exist without the experiences and support of my team at Ambition Data. Thank you to everyone who helped me apply these ideas over long hours and many years, especially **Loren Hadley**, **Michael Williamson**, **Jack Hulbert**, and **Lori Mayberry**.

Thank you to my analytics mentors **Gary Angel**, **Bob Page**, **Pete Fader**, **Sarah Toms**, and **Dan McCarthy** for your inspiration as well as my thought leadership mentors **Alison Harris** and **Denise Brosseau**. Without you, I would not have moved past my hesitations.

Thank you to my family, especially my husband **Hunt Wornall** who stepped up to leave his own career so I could focus on mine. To my boys Connor and Logan, you have made my world rich in all dimensions. Thank you to my mother, Judy, who never let an improper use of English slide by.

Turning an idea into a book is easier said than done. Thanks to **Heather Samarin** who pointed me in the right direction at exactly the right time, and to **Vanessa Campos** and **Jennifer Dorsey** at Broad Book Group for making this dream a reality.

Finally, to all those who have been such a special part of my journey: **Shani Trudgian**, **Kim Kralowec**, **Kim Rosengren**, **Michelle Gessaro**, **Diana Potts**, **Renee Alexander**, **Betsy Hadley** and all my podcast guests. You've inspired me again and again.

May the rising tide of customer-centricity lift all our boats.

ABOUT THE AUTHOR

Allison's experience and passion for analysis allow her to see future trends and relate it all the way back to the tactical moves her clients need to make today. She has built and executed digital customer analytics strategies for Fortune 500 customers including Nike, BlackRock, New England Biolabs, GlaxoSmithKline, HP, Intel, Microsoft, and Seagate as well as fast DTC companies including Dagne Dover, Paul Fredrick, and Xero Shoes.

Before Ambition Data, Allison was Senior Manager at Ernst & Young and VP Analytics at digital measurement firm Semphonic. Allison led several of Semphonic's largest engagements. Prior to that, Allison cofounded iSyndicate in San Francisco. iSyndicate was backed by Draper, Fisher, Jurvetson and sold digital content to Fortune 500 corporations from media publishers. Allison led the operations team and then the international team, where she opened iSyndicate's first European office in London and later struck a 50-50 joint venture with media powerhouse Bertelsmann.

Allison is published in *Forbes*, *MIT Technology Review*, and *Fast Company*. She has hosted the Customer Centricity Conference at Wharton and was recently named one of the Top 100 Women in Technology by Analytics Insight Magazine. You can listen to her interviews with successful customer-centric executives on her podcast, the **Customer Equity Accelerator**, via Apple Podcast, Stitcher, Google Play, Alexa's TuneIn, iHeartRadio or Spotify.

Outside of work, Allison has climbed Mt. Kilimanjaro, bicycled across the US, and rocked a number of local trivia competitions.

INDEX

SOURCES

INTRODUCTION

Davenport, Thomas H., and Jeanne G. Harris. *Competing on Analytics: The New Science of Winning*. Boston (MA): Harvard Business Review, 2017.

Indap, Sujeet. "What Happens in Vegas... The Messy Bankruptcy of Caesars Entertainment." *Financial Times*, September 26, 2017. https://www.ft.com/content/a0ed27c6-a2d4-11e7-b797-b61809486fe2

O'Keeffe, Kate. "Real Prize in Caesars Fight: Data on Players." *Wall Street Journal*, March 19, 2015. https://www.wsj.com/articles/in-caesars-fight-data-on-players-is-real-prize-1426800166

Schlappig, Ben. "Which Airlines Offer Escorts Through Security in The US?" One Mile At A Time, June 11, 2015. https://onemileatatime.com/which-airlines-offer-escorts-through-security-in-the-us/

Solomon, Micah. "How Zappos Delivers Wow Customer Service On Each And Every Call." *Forbes*, September 15, 2018. https://www.forbes.com/sites/micahsolomon/2018/09/15/the-secret-of-wow-customer-service-is-breathing-space-just-ask-zappos/?sh=22e09b11b2cf

Statista Research Department. "Number of social network users worldwide from 2017 to 2025." Statista, September 10, 2021. https://www.statista.com/statistics/278414/number-of-worldwide-social-network-users/

Kemp, Simon. "More Than Half of the People on Earth Now Use Social Media." Datareportal, July 21, 2020. https://datareportal.com/reports/more-than-half-the-world-now-uses-social-media

Carroll, Dave. "United Breaks Guitars." YouTube. July 6, 2009. Video, 4:36. https://www.youtube.com/watch?v=5YGc4zOqozo

Kleiner Perkins. "2015 Internet Trends." Kleiner Perkins, May 25, 2015. https://www.kleinerperkins.com/perspectives/2015-internet-trends

Binder, Christof and Hanssens, Dominique M. "Why Strong Customers Relationships Trump Powerful Brands." *Harvard Business Review*, April 14, 2015. https://hbr.org/2015/04/why-strong-customer-relationships-trump-powerful-brands?utm_source=eml&utm_medium=signal&utm_content=bullet1.

Choe, Anthony. "Customer Equity Accelerator - Episode 19: Customer as the Asset with Anthony Choe." Maximizing CLV with Anthony Choe, Founder of Provenance, May 2, 2018. https://customerequityaccelerator.podbean.com/e/ep-19-the-customer-as-the-asset-with-anthony-choe-founder-at-provenance-digital/

McCarthy, Dan. "Customer Equity Accelerator - Episode 15: Customer-Based Corporate Valuation." Using Data to Synthesize Marketing and Finance with Dan McCarthy, Assistant Professor of Marketing at Emory University, April 9, 2018. https://customerequityaccelerator.podbean.com/e/ep-15-customer-based-corporate-valuation-with-dan-mccarthy-emory-university/

Colmenares, Jaime. "Customer Equity Accelerator - Episode 10: Product v. Customer Centricity." Customer-Centric vs. Product-Centric Thinking with Jaime Colmenares, Former Director of Americas Customer Strategy & Analytics at eBay, March 2, 2018. https://customerequityaccelerator.podbean.com/e/ep-10-product-centricity-v-customer-centricity/

CHAPTER 3

Mesenbrink, John. "Going bolder: Up close with Kohler's president & CEO, David Kohler." *Plumbing Perspective*, June 12, 2017. https://plumbingperspective.com/going-bolder-up-close-with-kohlers-president-ceo-david-kohler

"Does Kohler Warranty Items Purchased Through Amazon?", Amazon, December 5, 2013. https://www.amazon.com/ask/questions/Tx28YJE69LJ96Q5?_encoding=UTF8&sort=helpful

Angel, Gary. "Customer Equity Accelerator - Episode 46: Measuring Offline Customer Experiences." Customer Accelerator Equity Accelerator Podcast, November 8, 2018. https://customerequityaccelerator.podbean.com/e/ep-46-measuring-offline-customer-experiences-with-gary-angel/

Winton, Peggy. "Customer Equity Accelerator - Episode 25: Transformation of Marketing Around CLV." How AIIM International Became Customer-Centric with Peggy Winton, President and CEO of AIIM International, June 13, 2018. https://customerequityaccelerator.podbean.com/e/ep-25-transformation-of-marketing-around-clv-with-peggy-winton/

CHAPTER 4

The Editors of Encyclopedia Britannica. "Nike, Inc." Britannica. https://www.britannica.com/topic/Nike-Inc

Baudey, Pierre-Laurent. "The Business of Platforms - Episode 19: On Driving Brand Growth, with Pierre-Laurent Baudey on Stitcher." The Business of Platforms with Pierre-Laurent Baudey on Stitcher, September 18, 2019. https://www.stitcher.com/show/the-business-of-platforms/episode/63207264.

Nike. "Nike, Inc. Acquires Data Analytics Leader Zodiac." Nike, March 22, 2018. https://news.nike.com/news/nike-data-analytics-zodiac

Peng, Matt. "5 More Nike Executives Are Out Amid Inquiry Into Harassment" *New York Times*, May 8, 2018. https://www.nytimes.com/2018/05/08/business/nike-harassment.html

Donahoe, John. "Nike Investor Annual Meeting," September 17, 2020. 2020 Nike Annual Shareholders Meeting.

Genter, JT. "American Airlines' Secret Passenger Scoring System Revealed." The Points Guy, January 8, 2018. https://thepointsguy.com/2018/01/american-airlines-secret-pax-score/

Davidson, Paul and Menton, Jessica. "Wells Fargo to pay $3B settlement for violating antifraud rules, resolving fake account probes." *USA TODAY*, February 21, 2020. https://www.usatoday.com/story/money/2020/02/21/wells-fargo-settlement-bank-reaches-3-billion-settlement-feds/4835436002/

Acosta, Danette. "Average Customer Retention Rate by Industry." ProfitWell. https://www.profitwell.com/customer-retention/industry-rates

Ambition Data. "How to Set-up a Testing Program." Customer Accelerator Equity Accelerator Podcast, May 2, 2019. https://www.ambitiondata.com/podcast/customer-equity-accelerator-podcasts-ep-69-how-to-set-up-a-testing-program-with-loren-hadley-at-ambition-data/

Hadley, Loren. "Customer Equity Accelerator - Episode 69: How to Set-up a Testing Program." Customer Accelerator Equity Accelerator Podcast, May 2, 2019. https://customerequityaccelerator.podbean.com/e/ep-69-how-to-set-up-a-testing-program-with-loren-hadley-at-ambition-data/

Banbury, Greg. "Customer Equity Accelerator – Episode 101: Customer-centric growth with NakedWines.com." How Naked Wines Became Customer-Centric with Greg Banbury, Cofounder of Naked Wines, December 12, 2019. https://customerequityaccelerator.podbean.com/e/ep-101-customer-centric-growth-with-nakedwinescom/

CHAPTER 5

Anderson, Zach. "Customer Equity Accelerator – Episode 15: CLV Transformation with Zach Anderson of Electronic Arts (EA)." Customer Accelerator Equity Accelerator Podcast, April 12, 2018. https://customerequityaccelerator.podbean.com/e/ep-16-clv-transformation-with-zack-anderson-of-electronic-arts-ea/

Roemmele, Brian. "Why Is The Starbucks Mobile Payments App So Successful?" *Forbes*, June 13, 2014. https://www.forbes.com/sites/quora/2014/06/13/why-is-the-starbucks-mobile-payments-app-so-successful/?sh=22437d273957

W3 Lab. "How Gillette's Ad Helped Dollar Shave Club." W3 Lab, November 7, 2019. https://w3-lab.com/gillettes-ad-dollar-shave-club/

Schrage, Michael. "What Most Companies Miss About Customer Lifetime Value." *Harvard Business Review*, April 18, 2017. https://hbr.org/2017/04/what-most-companies-miss-about-customer-lifetime-value

Halverson, Nate. "How social casinos leverage Facebook user data to target vulnerable gamblers." PBS, August 13, 2019. https://www.pbs.org/newshour/show/how-social-casinos-leverage-facebook-user-data-to-target-vulnerable-gamblers

Burt, Andrew. "New AI Regulations Are Coming. Is Your Organization Ready?" *Harvard Business Review*, April 30, 2021. https://hbr.org/2021/04/new-ai-regulations-are-coming-is-your-organization-ready

Saxena, Barkha. "Quantifying The Value Of A Data Organization: A Tale of Two Axes." *Forbes*, January 3, 2020. https://www.forbes.com/sites/forbestechcouncil/2020/01/03/quantifying-the-value-of-a-data-organization-a-tale-of-two-axes/

Murillo, Jose. "Customer Equity Accelerator – Episode 14: Delivering Massive Value with Analytics." How to Secure Budget for Customer-Centric Projects with Jose Murillo, Chief Analytics Officer at Banorte Bank, March 26, 2018. https://customerequityaccelerator.podbean.com/e/ep-101-customer-centric-growth-with-nakedwinescom/

Saxena, Barkha. "Customer Equity Accelerator – Episode 110: Scaling a Startup with Data, Barkha Saxena, Poshmark CDO." How Poshmark Leads a Customer-Centric Culture with Barkha Saxena, CDO of Poshmark, April 9, 2020. https://customerequityaccelerator.podbean.com/e/ep-110-scaling-a-startup-with-data-barkha-saxena-poshmark-cdo/

CHAPTER 6

Business Roundtable. "Business Roundtable Redefines the Purpose of a Corporation to Promote 'An Economy That Serves All Americans.'" August 19, 2019. https://www.businessroundtable.org/business-roundtable-redefines-the-purpose-of-a-corporation-to-promote-an-economy-that-serves-all-americans

B The Change. "Dear Business Roundtable CEOs: Let's Get to Work." B The Change, August 25, 2019. https://bthechange.com/dear-business-roundtable-ceos-lets-get-to-work-25f06457738c

Deiotte, Jim. "Customer Equity Accelerator – Episode 129: Next Generation Business Metrics with Jim Deiotte." The New Board Metrics: Environmental Social and Governance (ESG) with Jim Deiotte, Executive Director of the Master of Professional Accountancy Program at the University of California, December 17, 2020. https://customerequityaccelerator.podbean.com/e/ep-110-scaling-a-startup-with-data-barkha-saxena-poshmark-cdo/

CPSIA information can be obtained
at www.ICGtesting.com
Printed in the USA
BVHW032030040122
625470BV00014B/227